THE GREATEST

DEPRESSION OF

ALL TIME

Will America Survive This Time
&
What Can You Do About It

Don Braby

Table of Contents

Acknowledgments

It's amazing what it takes to write a book. I have a great admiration for all authors that undertake such a task. I also appreciate all those that spend countless hours of editing and critiquing manuscripts. Special thanks to my editor, Kurt Florman at www.proof-it.com for his work. Also, this book would not have been written without the help of my friends Dave Downey, who is an accomplished writer in his own right, Mary Scollard and Truly Griffin for their expertise. Special thanks to Jay for the cover photo: http://www.freephotos.com/index.php?photoid=14 033&action=viewphoto

Foreword

In my first book, ***The Approaching Winter: The Next Great Depression*** (Arthur House, 2005), I predicted a coming economic depression that would be the deepest and hardest of all time. In the book, I wrote about a number of reasons why the United States was about to enter an era of extreme hardship and an economic crisis unequaled by any other depression in the history of the world. I write this book, ***The Greatest Depression,*** as a sequel to the first.

The following is the foreword from my first book. *"**The Approaching Winter: The Next Great Depression** is a book that combines U.S. history and America's ever repeating cycles with a psychology that has been slowly changing form since the turn of the century. Within the next few years, America will have to come to grips with an approaching economic winter that could result in the worst depression in its 230 years of history. What we thought our children's children would have to struggle through may be ours to endure.*

As this book was being published by Author House, Americans experienced yet another great tragedy upon our soul as Hurricane Katrina ripped through the Gulf of Mexico coastline. This catastrophe, 9/11 and perhaps future events may be the triggers that will usher in the next great depression.

　　*As you read **The Approaching Winter: The Next Great Depression**, it may cause you to be fearful, angry and uncertain of our future. However, by reading this book you may be able to prepare yourself psychologically and perhaps economically to face the stormy and bitterly cold winter that awaits each and every one of us."*

　　As I begin writing this book, the approaching historic crisis, not realized by those that should know (government leaders) may have already begun. Most people do not realize just how deep the economic problems are. Some are calling for the possibility of a recession while others believe the economy is just going through a correction before it continues to expand into the next decade.

　　Many Americans are already in a recession as I finish this book in August 2008, and to them any talk from our leaders about the economy being strong is looked upon as government ignorance. The tremendous debt America has right now is staggering. And the most likely event that will trigger the greatest depression of all time will be the crash of the Dow Jones and other equity markets around the world.

　　This second book was written to help you, your family and friends survive the approaching economic winter that will come to be known as the Greatest Depression of all time in future history books.

Chapter 1

History, Cycles and The Bear Market

As Americans, we truly are a blessed people. Most of us have everything we want. We have the best jobs in the world. We have the best cars. We have the best homes. Ours is the highest standard of living enjoyed since the creation of the world. In the roaring '90s, we witnessed the longest economic expansion in the history of the United States as well as a bull market unequaled since this country was founded. Life has been grand. Talk of a New Era or a New Economy was widespread late in the decade. Financial prophets proclaimed prosperity for everyone. In 2003 and 2004 both the stock market and the economy recovered from the mini-recession of 2001 and established a positive upward trend.

In my first book, ***The Approaching Winter***, the following questions were asked for the reader to ponder: *"Will this trend continue? Better yet, can it? Can the United States continue an endless ascension into greater and greater prosperity? Or are we destined to repeat the same patterns and* *cycles of history? And can we catch a glimpse of our future if we cast but a glance at our past?"* These questions are slowly being answered as the economy is on the verge of entering a recession. The end of prosperity may well turn into the beginning of hardship for many.

United States History Points To Our Future

Our country's history shows very clearly that after every major economic expansion a major correction follows. In the Roaring Twenties, an enormous stock market rise and economic boom gave way to the Great Depression. The middle of the 19th century also saw an expansion followed by a depression. In fact, if we examine the totality of our history, dating all the way back to Independence, we find that a cycle repeats itself on the average every 75 years; every 75 years or so, the United States plunges into a crisis that lasts several years—sometimes as long as 20.

The first such crisis was the American Revolutionary War in 1780. The second was the Civil War in 1860. And the third was the Great Depression, which began in 1930. Are we about to enter a fourth era of extreme hardship?

The Roaring Twenties

Before answering that question, perhaps we ought to tackle this one: Does history really repeat itself? In our quest for the answer, let us consider the following, very telling quotes about the America of the 1920s.

1. *"There will be no interruption of our permanent prosperity."* Myron E. Forbes, President, Pierce Arrow Motor Car Co., January 12, 1928.[1]

2. *"No Congress of the United States ever assembled, on surveying the state of the Union, has met with a more pleasing prospect than that which appears at the present time... and the highest record of years of prosperity."* Calvin Coolidge, December 4, 1928.[2]

3. *"In most of the cities and towns of this country, this Wall Street panic will have no effect."* Paul Block, President of the Block newspaper chain, editorial, November 15, 1929.[3]

4. *"Stocks have reached what looks like a permanently high plateau."* Irving Fisher, Professor of Economics, Yale University, 1929.[4]

Now let's fast-forward to 1966 and examine the words of Alan Greenspan, one of the foremost financial officials of our time. This is what he said was the cause of the Great Depression:

"The excess credit which the Fed pumped into the economy spilled over into the stock market—triggering a fantastic speculative boom. Belatedly, Federal Reserve officials attempted to sop up the excess reserves and finally succeeded in breaking the boom. But it was too late: by 1929 the speculative imbalances had become so overwhelming that the attempt precipitated a sharp retrenching and a constant demoralizing of business confidence. As a result the American economy collapsed." [5]

Sounds a lot like 2005-2006, doesn't it? Observers could just as easily suggest the Fed had pumped so much credit into the economy that it spilled into the housing market and triggered another speculative boom. It's hard to believe that, after promoting several years of "easy money" or "easy credit," the former Federal Reserve chairman doesn't seem to remember what he said back in 1966.

Will today's excess credit trigger the same phenomenon history recorded of the 1920s and 1930s? It has often been said that if you don't learn from your mistakes you will repeat them over and over. The Roaring Twenties was famous for its excessive indulgence, something that has come to define the 1990s and today as well. Compare the events of those very different—yet

8

very similar—periods, and it becomes unmistakably clear: History is beginning to repeat. As we continue to explore this very disturbing reality, let's take a look at some of the key events of those Roaring Twenties.

<u>June 5, 1920</u>: Passage of the oil and coal land-leasing act lays the foundation for the biggest Washington scandal of the decade.

<u>March 6, 1922</u>: Babe Ruth signs a three-year contract with baseball's New York Yankees for a salary of $52,000 a year, the highest salary for a ballplayer up to then.

<u>March 25, 1922</u>: Women's fashions, with hemlines to the knee and beyond, are deemed so revealing that Catholic Pope Pius XI urges a campaign against them.

<u>May 10, 1924</u>: J. Edgar Hoover is appointed director of the scandal-plagued Bureau of Investigation (later renamed the FBI) with the charge of restoring the agency integrity and effectiveness.

<u>Sept 10, 1924</u>: The trial of the decade: Nathan Leopold, 19, and Richard Loeb, 18, who kidnapped and murdered a 14-year-old boy on May 22 for sport, are sentenced to life in prison. The case was noted for the murderers' cold lack of

remorse and because that they had come from a privileged background and had excelled in academics.

<u>Nov. 7, 1924</u>: A stock market boom that began early in the decade hits a five-year high with 2.33 million shares traded on the New York Stock Exchange.

<u>Dec 7, 1927</u>: U.S. Senate refuses to seat senator-elect Frank Smith from Illinois because the $485,000 he spent on his campaign was deemed unethically high. Two days later the same thing happens to senator-elect William Vare of Pennsylvania.[6]

Simply put, history repeats itself because people repeat history. America is about to repeat a very dark part of its history because those that lead our country are making the same type of mistakes leaders made in the Twenties. It is inevitable. America is about to enter a crisis that will turn out to be the deepest depression in our history. Why will it be the deepest? Because it is we who are enjoying the highest standard of living the world has ever seen. It is we that have so far to fall.

Things that will destroy America

Furthermore, it is interesting to note that in the early 1900s former President Theodore Roosevelt suggested, "The things that will destroy America are prosperity at any price, peace at any price, safety first instead of duty first, the love of

10

soft living, and the get rich quick theory of life."[7] As a nation we are fulfilling Roosevelt's prophecy. The government is determined to make the current level of prosperity as permanent as possible, no matter what the cost. That is at least partly why our leaders are spending billions of dollars to keep the peace around the world. (Of course, some would say we've spent billions making new enemies and poking our noses into other people's business.) Also, we Americans are driven to find ways to increase our already high standard of living and to retire with a sizeable nest egg. Of course, who wouldn't want that? The problem is, as Roosevelt foresaw, "the love of soft living and the get rich quick theory of life" is not healthy for the nation. It tends to create an even more lopsided imbalance between rich and poor. If America continues down this road, she may become a Third World country with no middle class in less than a decade.

Cycles That go Round and Around

Life is a cycle: We are born. At age five or six we start attending school. Most of us go on to graduate from high school. Some of us attend college. Many marry and raise families. We work most of our lives, hoping to retire in comfort. And yes, then we die. The cycle of life is something we accept and understand just as we do the seasons of the year. I will never forget those widely varying

11

seasons I experienced growing up in Iowa. We had bitterly cold winters, rainy and stormy springs, hot and muggy summers, and beautiful, cool autumns. The cycles of climate and life are very understandable and easy to predict. Not so, business and economic cycles. Those are tough even for experts to get their hands around. Economists tend to be wrong more than they are right.

Therefore, a key to understanding economics is the business cycle, a period of economic expansion followed by economic contraction. For the most part, the peak of each expansion occurred every three to five years between World War II and 1982. However, the period lasting from 1983 to 2000 was interrupted by a short economic contraction during 1990–1991. And since 2000, President Bush managed to avoid a major recession and win re-election in November 2004 by lowering the overnight interest rates and slashing taxes. On the surface, it may sound like Bush is a genius when it comes to mastering the economy. But there is a problem: The minor recession of 2001 did not fully correct the imbalances that have only grown larger as a result of Bush's financial policies.

The bottom line is that the contractions of the last 25 years have been nowhere near normal. Expansions are being forced to last longer and contractions are being artificially shortened by the Federal Reserve's actions, such as its manipulation of the overnight interest rate. When the Fed controls the rate instead of letting it flow naturally, as in a free market, bigger bubbles develop and those trigger bigger crashes. The Federal Reserve is creating a sort of perfect storm because it has been reacting to economic conditions instead of allowing for the proper flow of the normal business cycle.

Most economists break down economic cycles in months, years or decades. However, William Strauss and Neil Howe, in their book *The Fourth Turning,* show us a different type of cycle. They write about a cycle that has four seasons like our climate called turnings.

"The **First Turning** is a High (spring), an upbeat of strengthening institutions and weakening individualism, when a new civic order implants and the old value regime decays.

"The **Second Turning** is an Awakening (summer), a passionate era of spiritual upheaval, when the civic order comes under attack from a new value regime.

"The **Third Turning** is an Unraveling (fall), a downcast era of strengthening individualism and weakening institutions, when the old civic order decays and the new value regime implants.

"The **Fourth Turning** is a Crisis (winter), a decisive era of secular upheaval, when the value regime propels the replacement of the old civic order with a new one."[8]

According to the authors, each of these turnings lasts about 20 years—the length of a generation. One cycle of four turnings roughly matches the span of a human life. If you live to be 80 or 85, chances are you will live through a complete cycle. As well, each turning blends into the next one, as our climatic seasons do. As we make the transition from spring to summer, we have weeks of cool days mixed with warm ones. Temperatures do not soar from 40 degrees to 90 degrees in one day and stay there. Similarly, there is a transition period between one turning and the next. The time it takes to travel from one turning to the next is three to five years.

The authors also say there are four different types of generations, and those help determine what type of turning will occur at any particular time. According to Strauss and Howe, "at the start of each turning, people change how they feel about themselves, the culture, the nation, and the future. Each turning comes with its own identifiable mood. These mood shifts can catch people by surprise."[9]

Furthermore, as each generation comes and goes, so comes a new turning. In recent history, the first turning, which was a time of celebration, reigned from 1946 to 1964. As a country, we were coming off a tremendous victory in World War II. The industrial age was alive and well. Optimism was soaring throughout the nation. Even the sky was not the limit. In the early 1960s, President John F. Kennedy proclaimed that we would reach the moon by the decade's end, which, of course, would turn out to be true. But all that optimism came to a screeching halt with his assassination. His death ushered in the second turning, which Strauss and Howe call "The Awakening"—a twenty-year period from 1964 to 1984.

During that time, a new mood of negativity, rebellion and hatred descended like a dark cloud over the United States. From the Vietnam War to the hippie movement to the Beatles on the Ed Sullivan Show, signs were abundant that a new turning had arrived. This one would spawn the feminist, environmental and other political movements that would play major roles in shaping our society. The turning also triggered sharp increases in crime and divorce rates, and it happened to occur during the last major bear market.

Then the third turning arrived. We accepted the changes that took place in the second turning and moved on. In 1984, the shift to a new season was perhaps illustrated best by Apple Computer's Super Bowl commercial showing a young lady sledge-hammering 1950s stone-faced men on a large video screen. This was a knockout blow to Big Blue—the IBM mainframe—and the birth of the personal computer age.

Also born at that time was the individualism era, which Strauss and Howe call the "Unraveling." By the mid-1990s it had become clear that the cornerstone of American society— the family—was deteriorating. "In 1984, Americans were first noticing that the conventional family was no longer the norm and premarital teen sex no longer a rarity. A decade later, married couples with children had shrunk to only 26 percent of all households (versus 40 percent in 1970), and the share of sexually active fifteen-year-old girls had swollen to 26 percent (versus 5 percent in 1970)."[10]

From early 2008 to about 2010, the pace of the unraveling will increase as we enter twenty years of winter—the next major, long-lasting crisis.

The Bear Market

In early 2005, the Dow Jones appeared as if it was topping or slowing rolling over and beginning another bear market. However, investors remained optimistic because the Dow stayed above 10,000. Not only did the Dow march aggressively above its previous top, which was 11,750, it exploded to above 14,000 in October 2007. As the current bear market continues, the Dow Jones and all markets (domestic and worldwide), will begin to roll over much like a cresting ocean wave. During the growing momentum of a wave, there comes a time when water can rise no higher. As forces decrease and no longer are effective against the always-present and formidable pressure of gravity, the crest arrives and the wave crashes down. As for the waves rolling through the financial ocean, the Dow Jones and other markets may have already passed their crests in the fall of 2007. If not, they will crest very soon. Greed and the desire to buy more stocks fueled the rally that began in 2003, but fear and panic will trigger a major sell-off and a crash of equities in the next few years. As market prices fall, the investing world will be rocked by another wave of business scandals. When production numbers start to decrease, business men and women tend to let their emotions take over. To satisfy stockholders, business leaders make irrational, foolish decisions that eventually force them to "cook" their books. As stock prices rise, "Don't rock the boat," is the theme song at the company's staff meeting. The whistleblower is never welcomed. But when stocks plummet, tough questions are asked about the balance sheet and income statement.

Due to this fraud, new companies will rise up to take the unenviable place of Enron, MCI World Com, Tyco, and Arthur Andersen. The remains of these corrupt companies will be devoured by others the way vultures dine on what's left of a bear's kill.

The most widely known bear market in the United States lasted from 1929 to 1932. I will write more on this later, but it was primarily caused by investors and common people buying stocks on margin—banks lent out 50–90% cash that gave investors the opportunity to purchase additional stocks; (Sounds just like what happened to real estate from 2003–2006 as banks and lenders didn't really care about borrowers' credit.

Thousands of people were allowed to buy their dream homes with no money down). In October of 1929, the market collapsed and didn't return to its previous high for more than twenty years. The result of the '29 crash was the beginning of the Great Depression.

Many economists are of the opinion that a bear market begins when two or more indexes like the Dow Jones and S&P 500 fall 20% from their previous highs. Some market gurus believe a 15% fall justifies the declaration of a bear market. Stock technicians look for signs from the indexes themselves. A change from a bull market to a bear market is always an alert of extreme importance to the statistician. When a lower high coupled with a lower low occurs, technicians tend to predict that a bear market is highly probable. The first sign of a bear market is a weakening economy, which usually is characterized by lower disposable income, a higher unemployment rate, and a decline in corporate and business profits. Then as indexes' prices continue to fall, the economy will eventually contract into a recession. Once a bear market has begun, many investors lose 50–100% of their investments. As the bear market continues, good news—economic, political or domestic—has no real upward effect on the major indexes. Prices usually go sideways or fall. And bad news brings only lower prices. In bear markets like the infamous one of the 1930s, a continuation of fear and panic causes prices to tumble to lower and lower levels. The crash of 1929 didn't bottom until

July of 1932, and by then the value of the stock market had declined by 89 percent. Just as a bull market can produce an extreme optimism as prices overshoot their norm, a bear market will produce extreme pessimism and cause prices to undershoot the norm.

Then a turn begins. By that time, almost everyone is in the doom-and-gloom camp. Newspapers proclaim markets still have not bottomed and that the bottom is nowhere in sight. However, the markets treat this as the time to actually stop falling and put an end to the bear market. Good news is rewarded by an increase in rising prices for the major indexes. Bad news does not affect the markets very much at all. A higher high and a higher low are established. The economy may still look bleak with very little change having occurred in the unemployment rate or business profits, but a change has taken place nevertheless.

In fact, history tells us that lasting market bottoms tend to occur when the economy is still slipping, not when it's peaking. It was in August 1982 that the Dow Jones hit its last major bottom. On August 15 of that year, a *New York Times* article by William G. Shepherd Jr. titled "Dark Days on Wall Street" suggested the bear market of the early 1980s still had one more leg to go. "In the past two weeks," Shepherd wrote, "all the market averages have plunged to new lows as Wall Street, beset by cruel economic news from all sides, has time after time been unable to mount a sustained rally. That is a discouraging omen, an indication that the bottom has not been reached and a sign that even the most steel willed optimists may be about to throw in their towels." Shepherd went on, "The economic upturn is nowhere in sight. It did not appear in the second quarter of the year, as many people had hoped. It does not seem to be appearing in the third quarter either. Corporate profits are continuing to slide."[11]

Major market bottoms also tend to hit when no one is looking. According to Shepherd, several investors predicted the bottom in the Dow would strike somewhere between 550 and 650. Most thought for sure it would come at some number below 700. Like today's (2008) investor who is counting on the markets to continue their upward climb, the 1982 investor thought the bottom would never materialize. It did, however, on August 9, when the market hit 769.97. And guess what? No one was looking. It struck, in fact, six days before Mr. Shepherd's article was published, when "the economic upturn (was) nowhere in sight."

Since 1982 we have all seen an incredible advancement in all indices, including the Dow Jones, which went from that low in August of '82 to a high of 14,164 (closing) on October 9, 2007. Over the past quarter century, the value of Dow Jones stocks has soared by an astonishing 1,840%. But today's investors, homeowners, businessmen and women and politicians do not realize a bear market is about to devour them—one that will be so devastating it could be chronicled one day as the worst bear market in the history of the world. Are we about to repeat history once again? Yes! Unfortunately, Yes!

Chapter 2

The American Psyche

On Sept. 10, 2001, the last thing on Americans' minds was the potential for an attack to be launched on our soil from another country. That all changed, of course, the next day, when a pair of jumbo jets smashed through the glassy, metallic skin of the twin towers of the World Trade Center in New York City, and a third jet drilled into the Pentagon near the nation's Capitol. And we shall never forget the fourth jet that crashed in Pennsylvania after several heroic Americans tried to take over the plane. At that time, we rallied around our president as one. We took our flags out of our closets to show the world we stood behind our country. We prayed by candlelight for strength and for the comfort of those who had lost family and friends. For a while, this country was shaken to the point where it actually turned to God. But what has happened since that unforgettable day? What happened to that spirit of unity and of helping one another that was so widespread in the days and weeks after the tragedy?

What Has Happened to Our Thinking?

Sadly, many of us now are going on with life as if 9/11 never happened. We are beginning to forget the unforgettable. While those in New York and Washington, D.C. live with daily reminders, for many of us the attack is a distant memory. That is especially true of those who live in the Midwest and on the West Coast.

True, perhaps all of us will remember forever what time it was, where we were, and what we were doing when the unbelievable news reached our ears and eyes. Yet most of us continue to live just like we did before 9/11. Nothing, it seems, has changed.

But something *has* changed. We think and feel differently about ourselves, each other, our surroundings and our nation. Although invisible to many, an undeniable undercurrent of negativism and pessimism has taken root. Uncertainty, something we Americans are unaccustomed to dealing with, has pervaded our thinking. From the Iraq war to a struggling economy to the potential for another terrorist attack, we face an unknown future. Yes, we still have the largest economy on the planet and the world's most feared military force—two reasons why we've had an incredible economic expansion these last 5 years—but we are confronted with daunting new forces, including some we cannot see: forces of the mind.

Why the Nineteen-twenties are Like Today

Several years from now, historians will compare the '20s, which produced the Great Depression, to the first decade of the 21st century, which will have ushered in the Greatest Depression of all time. The overall psyche of the 1920s was shaped by a short-lived depression in 1921 that was similar in length only to a short-lived recession of 2001. Americans of the '20s also had a deeply imbedded desire for "things." The consumption of Americans during this period was the highest on record. A commercial of today that boldly says, "You got to have it," would have appealed to many care-free spending Americans of the '20s who were also addicted to spending their pay the moment they received it.

Years of Prosperity
The years 1923 through 1929 marked a time in our history when the nation's middle class not only expanded, but flourished with an ever-increasing standard of living. Prosperity was not a foggy dream anymore, but a lifestyle that that actually came true for many. Journalist Frederick

Lewis Allen wrote that this period represented "nearly seven years of unparalleled plenty... nearly seven years the prosperity bandwagon rolled down Main Street."[1] Shortly after the Great Crash of 1929 when Allen had more knowledge of the crash and its aftermath he thought this period was more about what we think and how we feel than of about a typical economic expansion. Allen stated, "Prosperity is more than an economic condition, it is a state of mind. The Big Bull Market had been more than a climax of a business cycle; it had been the climax of a cycle in American mass thinking and mass emotion. There was hardly a man or woman in the country whose attitude toward life had not been affected by it in some degree and was not now affected by the sudden and brutal shattering of hope. With the Big Bull Market gone and prosperity now going, Americans were soon to find themselves living in an altered world which called for new adjustments, new ideas, new habits of thought, and a new order of values. The psychological climate was changing; the ever-shifting currents of American life were tuning into new channels."[2]

Just as confidence in the system was important in the Twenties it is important now. The year 2008 marks the sixth year of continued economic expansion. Actually, had there not been the short-lived recession of 2001, the United States would be in a 16-year-long continual expansion dating back to 1992. Some suggest we did not really have a downturn in 2001, but only a minor slow down because the consumer continued to spend during this time. Unfortunately, due to the boom that persisted from 2003 through 2007, Americans are destined for a number of painful trials and hardships throughout the next decade: 2010–2020.

The Dow Jones

The Dow Jones is the most watched stock market index in the world. The blue chips are made up of 30 of the largest and most important companies in the United States. Furthermore, the Dow is like a barometer of how we feel and what we do. Sentiment and customer confidence are driven by the long-term direction or trend of the Dow Jones. On a typical day, billions of transactions occur on the New York Stock Exchange and in other markets around the globe. Investors make decisions every day that result in billions of dollars changing hands. And emotions play a major role in these decisions. When emotions such as greed and fear reign, markets behave wildly. We create manias, or bubbles, such as those of 1925–29 and 1995–2000, when greed is king. We create stock market crashes, such as in 1929–32, 1987, 2000-2002, when fear rules. Obviously, these two states of mind and their consequent behavior patterns are not healthy for the markets or the economy.

As the economy of 2008 continues to struggle and become deeply entrenched in a recession, the American psyche will become increasingly more pessimistic. Very soon Americans will be able to relate to our co-citizens of the 1930s. We will go through an array of emotions. First there will be surprise. Then we will see disbelief, shock, concern, fear, frustration, anger, outrage and, finally, depression. These emotions will trigger massive protests and marches in our nation's largest cities and our nation's capital. Unemployment will rise sharply. Real estate foreclosures and personal/corporate bankruptcies will continue to multiply and set records.

Why Booms and Crashes?

In looking back at our nearly 230-year history, several questions come to mind. Why has the United States had several booms and crashes? And what happens when amateurs become involved with these booms? Obviously, the answers are always clearer after bubbles burst. During the Roaring Twenties, investors—including amateurs—were making easy money hand over fist by playing the stock market. Then came the crash of 1929 and the deepest depression in U.S. history up to that time. Ninety-nine percent of the population did not expect anything like the stock market crash in late '29 and the depression that stung this country for most of the 1930s. Similarly, during the time my first book was published, the vast majority of people expected the stock market and housing prices to keep on rising. Stocks did extend higher through October 2007, but housing prices have fallen hard with no bottom in site. Modern investors also say nothing like 1929 and the Thirties will happen again anytime soon, either because we already have seen the big crash (2000–2002) of our generation or because a 1929-style crash is simply no longer possible. But that is precisely why it *will* happen.

However, in the early part of 2008, many people were reluctantly acknowledging that the economy had taken a turn for the worse. Former Federal Reserve Chairman Alan Greenspan estimated there was a 50/50 chance that a recession would be declared by the end of the year. But most Americans are in for a rude awakening because almost no one has imagined that another 1930s-type depression is even remotely possible. We will find ourselves relating to the tale about the frog in the pan of water on the stove. As the temperature rises to the boiling point, the frog does not realize it's in danger until it is too late. Neither will we. And like a deer caught in the glare of headlights, most of us will have no idea which way to turn.

The pressures of a credit collapse and an impending stock market crash will continue to build as we close out this decade. Most corporations will find it extremely difficult to keep pace with Wall Street's expectations. But why are we again repeating the Twenties, specifically 1929? Perhaps a quote from Scottish writer Charles Mackay, who was the author of "Extraordinary Popular Delusions and the Madness in Crowds," can shed some light. He writes, "Men, it has been well said, think in herds; it will be seen that they go mad in herds, while they recover their senses slowly, and one by one."[3]

Don't Follow the Crowd Now!

Americans love teams that win. That is why for many years the Dallas Cowboys of the National Football League were known as America's Team. In the 1990s, the Cowboys won three Super Bowls in four years. It also is why millions who rarely watch a baseball game tuned in to see if the Boston Red Sox would win a World Series for the first time in 86 years. When the Red Sox did, 3.2 million fans turned out for the victory parade. They wanted to show appreciation for their team. But perhaps more than that, they wanted to see the team that erased the curse. It took 86 years for the Boston Red Sox to finally win the last game of a season.

In short, Americans love to jump on the bandwagon. However, when it comes to investing, climbing aboard is not such a good idea at the end of the trail. When a large number of people, particularly novices, become involved with stock investment clubs or speculate in real estate, it's time to flee such investments. It's never a good sign for any investment vehicle when amateurs get involved. In my first book, ***The Approaching Winter: The Next Great Depression***, which was published in 2005, I wrote, *"When housing prices soar as fast and as high as they have been, it may seem like just about anyone can get rich in real estate. Those that are buying property now are simply blinded by the $$ signs in their eyes. All of us very soon will see that the numerous get-rich-quick real estate commercials on TV and radio these past few years are actually signaling the end of the housing bubble.*

"Home prices haven't seen a correction in 10 years. In fact, real estate prices decade to decade haven't declined since the 1930s. And the mercurial rise as of late is not a healthy sign for the future because droves of non-experts are buying homes as investments. People are taking advantage of the lowest mortgage interest rates in 40 years. And why shouldn't they? It's easy money courtesy of the United States government. Besides, everyone knows someone who has cashed in on an equity windfall. Many are convinced they must

climb aboard this bandwagon now or they will miss out."

I continued, *"Unfortunately, this kind of runaway real estate speculation is causing a herding effect. People are rushing to buy houses before interest rates creep back up and home prices shoot up even more. Just like a herd of stampeding cattle with no sense of direction, buyers are becoming more and more irrational in their thinking. Most don't care at all about the historically high prices. They just want a home. In the case of investment property, a second home, many home owners are not concerned if they have a renter or not. These real estate investors are just banking on the continuing property value appreciation. Also, prospective buyers are so desperate for 'ownership' that they are willing to sign 40-year or interest-only mortgages. The sad reality is, these unfortunate people will be the first to turn their keys in to their bank."*

It is very obvious today that the bubble has popped and real estate prices are starting a freefall. Thousands of foreclosed homeowners are beginning to turn in their keys. In his book *According to Hoyt: Fifty Years of Homer Hoyt: 1916–1966,* Hoyt wrote that the extreme rise in the number of foreclosures in 1927 "was a barometer of approaching financial storms."[4]

As for stock investors, they will be growing increasingly anxious as markets continue their downward trend, and they will begin selling in earnest. The Dow Jones' inability to stay above support levels of 12,000, 10,600 and 10,000 will be the first alarm. Then more worry and fear will spread like gangrene as the Dow Jones begins to flail, falling below 9,000 initially, then 8,000. Once the 7,000 mark is breached, the herding phenomenon will continue to reverse as stock market and real estate prices plummet. Robert Prechter explains this in his book *The Wave Principle of Human Social Behavior and the New Science of Socionomics.* He says, "The error of optimism dies and gives birth to an error of pessimism."[5] This psychology is the primary ingredient of booms and crashes.

Simpler Times, Please

Countless times in my early years, while growing up on my family's dairy farm in Iowa, I would ponder how fortunate I was to live in a nation that provided so much freedom and opportunity. I remember spending countless hours daydreaming about my future—I wanted to be a professional football player. And if not that, I wanted to be the first person to walk on the red planet, Mars. There were two reasons for that. My favorite football team, the Green Bay Packers, had just won the first two Super Bowls. And the

United States had just put the first man on the moon.

The year was 1969. I was 12 years old. Life was simple, especially for a boy on a Midwest farm. No one was in a hurry. And if you met someone on a gravel road you always waved, no matter who it was—neighbor, friend, or total stranger. Almost everyone was a Sunday driver. Traveling from Garden Grove to Dallas Center to visit Grandma seemed to take forever. It didn't help that my older sisters bored me to death, counting horses as we drove Highways 69 and 6, and Interstate 35. Iowa, with its lush green vegetation and beautiful rolling hills, was truly the best place in the world to grow up. Life was so simple, so easygoing.

My parents were as conservative as you could get, as they themselves had been raised during the Great Depression. The lessons they learned from their parents they passed on to my three sisters and me. However, over time those lessons became harder to remember and harder to implement. I do remember, though, in the late '70s while attending electronic school in West Des Moines, Iowa, and working part time, that I could save at least half my paycheck.

Life is so very different now—so complex and so difficult. Most of us feel like a ball in a pinball machine that is bounced all over the place, without any control of its own. Our jobs are like that. The demands we face seem to get more complex by the day. For many Americans, our homes have become a place only to rest for the night, rather than a place for spending an evening with a warm family in which members express genuine concern for each other. Where has the communication gone? Where have all the flowers gone?

Due to the current credit crisis and weakening economy, businesses throughout the United States have been taking great pains to cut costs in every company department for some time now. To make sure each department is performing at the highest possible level, managers are working longer hours to keep up with demands coming down from the top. As for the rest of us—we who actually do the work—we are doing two to three times what we did just five years ago.

But this is called productivity. Because of this added workload, life on the job has become infinitely more complicated and stressful. As of this writing, the economy is struggling so much that it is about to enter a recession. Company budgets will become extremely tight, forcing firms to lay off those they just hired. Many companies will demand remaining employees do more and more work. However, as jobs become scarce, employers will have the upper hand. As the economy continues to weaken over the next few years, most companies will try to squeeze more productivity out of their employees. Employees will have to adapt to still more demands. Still, companies will find it increasingly difficult to curb costs, and eventually they will ax jobs in huge numbers.

For that reason, your biggest asset is how well you do your job and how valuable you are to your employer. Be the best of the best. Give your boss many reasons for keeping you and zero reasons for letting you go. Hang in there. It is better to persevere under an increasing workload than to struggle financially while looking for another way to put food on the table.

So just why is today's world so complex? Will we ever get back to simpler times? Of course, there are several reasons why we live in a complex world. The main reason is at our fingertips: the computer. Because of the computer and the internet, far more information is available to us than at any other time in history. Innovation and technology keep delivering faster and smarter computers, which in turn deliver information at ever-increasing speeds. The computer also has provided a way for businesses to cut costs by going paperless, giving an employee all he or she needs to do his or her job through the click of a mouse.

It sounds simple, but only for those who can keep up. We have become overloaded with information. Therefore, I predict the expansion of the information age is about to run its course. Since technology is directly tied to information, the information age will dramatically wind down in the coming years.

How do I know this, you ask? Well, consider this. When companies and corporations report higher product inventories, combined with lower consumer spending, we have the beginnings of a business contraction. And that means lower profits. When businesses contract, every department gets its budget slashed, including the crucial research and development division. Less money in turn translates into less innovation and, in some cases, none at all. And less innovation means less information.

The world that we know is about to change forever. From crooked politicians to cooked corporate books to complicated job demands, Americans are about to say, "Enough is enough. We've had enough of this fast-paced, complicated, stressed-out world!"

Sooner or later we will get our way, but at what cost? The United States is on the verge of waking up to what really matters. For many of us, life will be reduced to having a job that pays only for the clothes on our backs, food on our tables, and roofs over our heads. The time is coming when we will consider a job that just takes care of the bare necessities to be a tremendous blessing. For many of us, a steady income will no longer be the trigger for ever-increasing greed but rather the difference between simply having a home and being homeless.

So what is wrong with America's psyche? Will we ever get back to simpler times, when we didn't have to think so much and when life wasn't so stressful? Will America survive the worldwide pessimistic trend that began in 2000 and 2001? I truly hope America will overcome the Greatest Depression of all time and experience a time like the 1950s when almost everyone was a Sunday driver.

The American psyche is clearly headed in the wrong direction. To turn us around, America will need a leader like Abraham Lincoln, who led this country to victory in the bloody Civil War and helped abolish slavery. The United States will need a leader like Franklin Roosevelt, who united this nation and helped Americans weather the Great Depression with his famous fireside chats. Together we will overcome. Together we will regain that spirit of unity, like we did in the days following 9/11. Before America hits bottom, we must come to our senses one by one and ask God for help like we did on Sept. 11, 2001.

Chapter 3

The Causes of The Next Great Depression

As in the Great Depression of the 1930s, Americans will be clamoring to know why and how another depression happened. We will have tons of questions, but few answers. We will have many opinions, but few will make sense.

In my first book I wrote, "*In my opinion, the causes of the next great depression will be clear: An unseen reversal in psychology from optimism to pessimism was the catalyst to a bear market in stock exchanges in 2000. Basic economics and common sense were abandoned as government leaders, in their insatiable thirst for power, ignored the warning signals of the largest national and personal debt in history and an extreme over-extension of credit. The bursting of the credit bubble, along with the crash of the stock and housing markets, ushered in fears of deflation and a contracting economy. And that will produce a downward spiral of despair and the greatest U.S. depression of all time.*"

The American Debt

It doesn't take a rocket scientist to realize America has a bad spending habit. According to the Grandfather Economic Report, on January 1, 2008, the federal debt that was actually reported stood at $9.2 trillion—an increase of $3.5 trillion since President Bush took office in 2001.[1] In just seven years, Mr. Bush and his administration have increased our debt by more than 62%. And by the time Bush finally leaves office the federal debt will reach almost $10,000,000,000,000. Of the $9.2 trillion, the United States owes foreign nations $2.4 trillion, the U.S. domestic public $2.7 trillion and trust funds $4.1 trillion.

As if that weren't enough, total household debt had skyrocketed to $13.8 trillion at the beginning of this year.[2] That figure includes $943.5 billion of revolving credit and $1.5 trillion [3] of non-revolving credit as well as $11.4 trillion in mortgage debt. Meanwhile, corporate debt has soared above $10.1 trillion for the first time.[4] All this adds up to a record U.S. debt that has gone unchecked for almost a decade now. Any way you slice it, the United States has become the single largest debtor in the world. But who is really responsible for just a large debt? Who has put us in this predicament? Well, let's take the $9.2 trillion federal debt and present the facts directly from www.treasurydirect.com. Just before Ronald

Regan was voted in as the 40th president of the United States in November 1980, the federal debt stood at $907 billion. When Bill Clinton was elected in 1992 the federal debt was $4.064 trillion. Under two Republican presidents, Reagan and George Bush Sr., from 1980 to 1992 the debt rose over 448%, or more than 4.48 times. Under President Clinton the federal debt rose 41% to $5.728 trillion. We all know what has happened to the federal debt under President George W. Bush: a 62% increase from $5.728 trillion to $9.395 trillion as of this writing. If we just compare the total amounts between Republican and Democrat presidents it's clear who has spent the most: the Republicans have outspent the Democrats $6.7 trillion to $1.6 trillion. True, we're just comparing totals and not total years. Also, the Republican presidents, due to their own decisions, had two major wars to fund: the Gulf War in 1991 and the Iraq War, which of course continues. However, even if we gave more presidential years (12) to the Democrats and at the same spending rate of President Clinton, the Republican presidents would still have outspent their rivals by more than 67%.

Furthermore, it's not just the sheer magnitude of our debt that is alarming. It's also disturbing how fast we are plunging ever deeper into the red personally. In just one year—2007—household debt shot up 8 percent, climbing by $1 trillion.[5] Making things worse, personal bankruptcies increased nearly 40 percent over last year; there were 573,000 in 2006 compared to 800,000 in 2007.[6] Even though this is far from the record of 2 million in 2005, which was the year the new U.S. bankruptcy laws were passed by Congress, many are predicting this trend to worsen due to the home mortgage debacle.

We don't have to look far to see where all this is going. On January 12, 2004, William Branigin of the *Washington Post* stated in an article that, "To some, the nation's consumer debt, which dwarfs that of any other country, represents the kind of 'bubble' that the stock market grew into during the 1990s."[7] Mr. Branigin also mentioned that the credit-card industry estimated the average household credit card balance at $9,000. Also, in October 2007, there were 26% more credit card owners at least 30 days late compared to October 2006.[8] The increase was again tied to the home mortgage crisis.

America, we have a problem. Why are we spending money we don't even have? What's the point of keeping up with the Joneses if we don't have a dime to our name?

Greenspan's Bluff Was a Very Bad Hand

Now, if you asked former Federal Reserve Chairman Alan Greenspan what he thought about all this debt, you received conflicting answers. Take for example a quote from a speech he delivered to the Economic Club of New York on March 2, 2004: "Can market forces incrementally defuse a worrisome buildup in a nation's current account deficit and net external debt before a crisis more abruptly does so?"[9] True, Mr. Greenspan did not specify that he was talking about the United States, but it sure seemed like he was. After all, we are the largest debtor nation in the world. However, in a speech to the Credit Union National Association a couple of days later, he suggested there was no threat of crisis as he stated, "Overall, the household sector seems to be in good shape."[10]

After reading both those quotes, it would appear that Mr. Greenspan had found a solution to all this debt. Or rather, that he had found the necessary trillions of dollars to fix the imbalances. Sorry to say, Mr. Greenspan had not. However, he still tried to convince us not to worry. On Oct. 26, 2004, before an organization called America's Community Bankers, Mr. Greenspan said, "Household finances appear to be in reasonably good shape."[11] On the other hand, he did suggest things could change if there was a sharp decline in housing prices and consumer paychecks. This is why Greenspan in early 2008 predicted that the United States had a 50 percent chance of entering a recession by the end of the year. From 2004–2006 though, Mr. Greenspan was hoping we wouldn't call his bluff. However, as Greenspan lays down his cards, we'll see he didn't even have a pair. He and President Bush should be held accountable by the American public for having started the next great depression.

The Housing Bubble

Over the last several years, I have come to realize that the economy lags behind the stock market four to twelve months. For example, although markets peaked in January and March of 2000, the mini-recession that followed did not get underway until January 2001. Likewise, the economic expansion we've enjoyed since late 2003 and throughout 2007 began after markets hit a temporary bottom in October 2002.

As far as real estate goes, housing prices typically start to fall two to three years after a major top in the stock market. This occurred in the 1930s, then again in 1989. However, real estate prices climbed steeply from 2002–2006 because of the lowest interest rates in more than forty years and the expanding credit bubble, courtesy of Mr. Greenspan and the Federal Reserve. The Fed overnight funds rate went from 6.5% in January 2001 to 1% in June of 2004. This 1% rate was kept in place for a whole year. In summer of 2007, however, a new downward trend emerged: lower housing prices and a contraction of credit. With the "easy money" policy of the Bush administration and the Federal Reserve, both the credit expansion and real estate prices were allowed to become overextended without limits (sub-prime mortgages, interest-only loans, adjustable-rate mortgages, etc.). Unfortunately, Bush's policy of "easy money" and the decisions that have been made since August of 2007 (more on that later) will only lead us to an economic collapse more dramatic and crippling than it should have been.

We have all known since we were children that what goes up must come down. As simple as that sounds, the very same principle applies to the stock and housing markets. Yet it is disturbing that we haven't seen a healthy correction in real estate prices for some time, in fact for more than a decade. Not only have prices continued to climb, this rise has fueled the same kind of speculation in the real estate arena that we saw in the stock market in the late 1990s. A March 2004 report by Bridgewater Associates, a money manager and institutional research firm from Connecticut, illustrates this genuine concern with the real estate bubble: "As with any unsustainable market, or economic event, it is impossible to pinpoint when the reversal is about to take place, but a pop in this bubble will likely have a larger affect on households than the popping of the NASDAQ did."[12] Furthermore, an article by Tom Kelly of STLtoday.com shows how much speculation is actually in the real estate market. An online survey by the National Association of Realtors revealed "that 23 percent of all homes purchased in 2004 were for investment, while another 13 percent were vacation homes." Mr. Kelly continued, "It now appears that the purchase of investment property and vacation homes accounts for more than one-third of residential transactions."[13]

It is interesting to note that, from 1995 to 2000, when the stock market was in its heyday, the NASDAQ climbed 44 percent per year. Similarly, from March of 2000 to June 2005, the stocks of home builders soared 46 percent each year.[14] Then in mid 2007, home building stocks started to fall off a cliff just as the NASDAQ did from 2000 to 2002. The following is a quote from my first book, *The Approaching Winter*. *"Furthermore, when investors lost money in the bear market of March 2000 to October 2002, many invested what they had left in real estate. This infusion of new money spurred prices to rise even higher. According to a report released in May 2005 by the California Association of Realtors (C.A.R.), the median price for a single family home in California was*

$509,230.[15] In June 2005, C.A.R. reported the affordability index, a percentage of households that can afford to purchase a median priced home, slid in April to 17 percent, a drop of 3 percent from a year ago. Obviously, with these outrageous prices many Americans are not able to buy a house.

"Looking at U.S. Census reports for the last two decades, median home values for the nation as a whole increased by an average 28 percent from 1980 ($93,400) to 2000 ($119,600).[16] Since 1940, there has never been a decade in which median prices dropped. We have to go all the way back to 1930 to find such a major correction in the real estate market.

"Now, let's fast forward to 2005. In April 2005, the national median existing-home price was $217,000, a stunning 81.5 percent increase since just the turn of the century.[17] It has taken a mere five years for prices to blaze well past the rate of increase for the previous 20 years. The bottom line is, this trend simply cannot be sustained much longer.

"In regards to local markets, Mr. Greenspan seems to agree. On June 9, 2005, Mr. Greenspan testified before the Joint Economic Committee of Congress that, 'Although a "bubble" in home prices for the nation as a whole does not appear likely, there do appear to be, at a minimum, signs of froth in some local markets

47

*where home prices seem to have risen to unsustainable levels.' But what do you call an 81.5 percent leap in the national median existing-home price in five years compared to a much more gradual 28 percent rise over two decades? You call it what it is—a **nation-wide real estate bubble that will burst within two or three years**. In fact, the decline of real estate prices will be like climbing down Mt. Everest without any ropes and via a descent that has never been attempted before. In others words a free-fall.*

"Of course, it didn't help that President Bush, in several 2004 campaign speeches, urged Americans to continue buying homes. He even promised some could achieve home ownership with no money down.[18] Ownership plus no money down equals bank-owned to me. Furthermore, we all know what our president's spending habits are like and how they have produced record deficits. And now he is encouraging us to take on still more debt. "I've got a question for you, Mr. President. When will all these bills be paid? The truth is, most will go unpaid. Many 'home owners' will default on loans and turn in keys to the bank. As interest rates surge higher, Americans will no longer be able to refinance their mortgages. And the resulting spending freeze will trigger the end of the real estate bubble.

"It is very clear why President Bush is pushing ownership. It is the one and only industry

that has kept this economy moving. And he knows it. Bush knows that when Americans stop buying homes and refinancing mortgages, they will also stop running down to Home Depot and Ikea to buy things for those new houses. Remember, we the people are 70 percent of the economy. And President Bush is determined to keep us spending. What the president doesn't seem to understand is that he is only pumping more air into the bubble."

The result of the housing bubble will produce a collapse not seen since the depression. This bubble became so huge that, as it continues to burst, real estate prices are going to plummet 60 to 90 percent in the coming deflation. And it's not like something similar hasn't happened before. Consider a case in point: In 1836, an acre of land in Chicago was fetching $11,000. By 1840, that same acre was being given away for a mere $100.[19] Also, we cannot forget that the real estate market has not had a substantial correction in more than 75 years.

Certainly, it is hard to believe that a house valued at $200,000 at the peak could be worth only $20,000 just a few years from now. But if history repeats itself, as I strongly believe it will, we will witness a precipitous drop in home prices. Many Americans need to prepare themselves to be upside down for the entire period covered by their mortgage. The value of your home may be so low that you'll just *give* it to one of your children when you pass away. The approaching winter will so shake our confidence that many of us will begin to realize there is more to life than climbing to the top of the corporate ladder, living in the biggest house on the block, and collecting the most toys. Many of us will desire a return to the values of the noble men and women that shaped this great country and won our independence in the late 1700s.

The Start of the Credit Bubble's Collapse

Here is another statement from my first book. *"In the book, **Conquer the Crash**, author Robert R. Prechter, Jr. says the collapse of the credit bubble must be preceded by a huge buildup in the extension of credit. We are talking about bank loans, corporate and consumer debt, credit card debt, and home mortgages. Mr. Prechter says, 'Near the end of a major expansion, few creditors expect default, which is why they lend freely to weak borrowers. Few borrowers expect their fortunes to change, which is why they borrow freely.' However, as Mr. Prechter continues, 'The expansion of credit ends when the desire or ability to sustain the trend can no longer be maintained.'[20] In other words, the lender stops lending because the borrower doesn't have the* *cash to pay back loans. And once the credit bubble starts to lose air, consumers will no longer have cash for buying appliances, furniture, equipment, cars, and houses. Simply put, consumers will stop consuming."*

Clearly, Mr. Prechter is correct. It is happening as I rewrite this chapter. Americans are growing a lot less confident about the stock market and overall economy. Many of us are actually spending our money more wisely. As the economy weakens we will start to buy just what we really need and not what we want. It won't be long before we are able to relate with cowboy comedian Will Rogers. In the book *Reflections and Observations* in 1932, Mr. Rogers mused, "Gosh, wasn't we crazy there for a while? Why the thought never entered our head that we wasn't the brightest, wisest, and the most accomplished people that was ever on this earth. Hadn't we figured out 'mass production'? Couldn't we make more things than anybody? Did the thought ever enter our bone head that the time might come when nobody would want all these things we were making? No, we had it all figured out that the more we made, the more they would want. Honest, as we look back now, somebody ought to have taken each one of us and soaked our fat heads. We bought everything under the sun, if they would sell it on enough installments."[21]

Back in the 1930s, consumers bought

merchandise by making monthly payments called installments. The longer the period covered by the installments, the more you could buy. Of course today we have credit cards and various types of loans. Against the backdrop of the lowest interest rates in 40 years, consumers are still bombarded weekly with offers to apply for credit cards. However, the spending spree is just about over. The time is coming when we will all start spending a lot less. And because consumer spending accounts for 70 percent of our nation's economy, the credit bubble will continue to deflate. Remember, credit does not equal cash; credit equals debt. In *The Approaching Winter*, I predicted the impending eruption of the credit bubble would be *"like a volcano that's ready to blow its top."*

What is the Federal Reserve to do?

So, do current Federal Reserve Chairman Bernanke and President Bush realize that a very long and bitter economic winter is upon us? Obviously, our leaders are highly educated and determined to do the best job that they can. But given that they are among the smartest people in the world, shouldn't Bush and Bernanke be able to prevent a major collapse of our economy and the greatest depression of all time? Again, I will call your attention to a paragraph in my first book, which at the time was directed at Mr. Greenspan and President Bush. *"It is not clear whether they know—however, even if they do know, they can't do anything about it. Raising and lowering interest rates won't do any good when the gigantic, hideous monster of debt cries out, 'Pay now!' The damage has already been done. The only hope our leaders have of staving off the burst is to keep the American public confident for as long as possible. But our confidence is on thin ice and a large number of Americans will be forced to endure a long and bitterly cold economic winter."*

If you think the Federal Reserve, which is one of the most powerful institutions in the world, controls the economy of this nation and therefore its destiny, you are right. Not only did the Fed create the housing and credit bubble by slashing interest rates to their lowest point in four decades, it has set the stage for the coming crash of the economy. Now, the Federal Reserve is trying to correct the mistakes it and the Bush administration made while Mr. Greenspan was chairman. Whatever they decide will create more problems. It will be like attempting to stop an avalanche that's half way down the mountain.

In an effort to prevent the United States from entering a recession, the Federal Reserve started lowering interest rates again, from 5.25% in September 2007 to 2% in April 2008. In addition to lowing rates—both the overnight and discount rate—the Fed injected hundreds of billions of dollars into the financial system in a bid to prop up the mortgage industry and to ease a worldwide credit contraction. Beginning in August 2007, the reserve added $62 billion to help financial institutions sell some of the $260 billion worth of U.S. unsold loans and another $200 billion[22] in Europe that no one wanted. Due to relaxed lending standards that produced the sub-prime crisis, these securities, which represented bad and good loans packaged by the hundreds, were losing value every day. This "buyers" strike stopped the mortgage machine in its tracks. The result: The beginning of a credit contraction that will affect every market in the world.

Furthermore, on March 11, 2008, the Federal Reserve pledged $200 billion of U.S. Treasuries in exchange for mortgage debt. In other words, a buyout was in the works. This, again, was meant to stabilize the financial markets that were in major trouble because of the credit contraction. To make matters worse, on March 14 the 85-year-old investment bank Bears Streans had to be rescued by J.P. Morgan for $30 billion, which was guaranteed by the government (A good old fashion bailout). Unfortunately for the Fed, Bear Streans is only the first of many. After all this it had become clear to the American public that the Fed had its hands full with the credit crisis. Mr. Bernanke and the committee members of the Federal Reserve are not only trying to avoid a deflation of the credit market, but the possibility of runaway inflation due to rising energy costs and the falling dollar.

Deflation, Stagflation or Hyper-inflation

Again, let's go back to my book *The Approaching Winter*. *"On April 20, 2004, Alan Greenspan said the 'D' word. Yes, he muttered the word that is feared and dreaded in economic circles: Deflation. In testifying on Capitol Hill, Greenspan said, 'It's fairly apparent that pricing power is gradually being restored and threats of deflation, which were a significant concern last year, by all indications are no longer an issue before us.'[23] One year earlier, he didn't have the stomach to say the word. On May 21, 2003, Mr. Greenspan spoke rather of an 'unwelcome substantial fall in inflation.'[24] Why is Mr. Greenspan so comfortable saying the word deflation now?: Because he had managed to re-inflate the economy since mid 2003. However, he and President Bush are between a rock and a hard place. They are going to have to make a choice between deflation and inflation. They are in a Catch-22."* Mr. Bernanke finds himself in the same place, but the stakes are a lot higher. And there is hardly any bubble left to inflate. True, with oil climbing above $145 per barrel and gold to more than $1,000 per ounce in the first half of 2008, one could argue the last bubbles are oil and gold—the commodities. Some are now predicting $200 oil and $2,500 gold. Does this remind you of any other bubble that many were claiming would continue forever?

So what are we going to have to endure, deflation, stagflation or hyper-inflation? The answer may lie in Basic Economics 101 and the most fundamental of economic theories: supply and demand. Years from now, when we look back on the causes of the Greatest Depression of all time, we will see that the American consumer did exactly what our government wanted us to do. We shopped until we dropped. We did as much as we could. Instead of charging four credit cards, we applied for four more. Instead of saving for a rainy day, we bought a new truck, a new entertainment system or a new house. Some of us bought a second house for investment purposes, believing that what went up would keep going up. Not to mention that President Bush encouraged us to do all this. He doled out tax refunds and gave us the opportunity to spend even more money. And his shop-'til-you-drop strategy left us with a terribly unbalanced government checkbook.

But as consumers are forced to cut back on their spending, demand will decrease, lowering prices. In turn, this will trigger an oversupply of products, driving down prices more. As the downward trend gains a foothold, look for several department and novelty store chains to file for bankruptcy and close their doors. This will leave still more products on the shelf, reducing prices still more. With more inventory shipments will decrease and that in turn will lower the overall demand for oil. If the troubling trend continues, Americans will be forced to start cutting back even more and look for ways to save. This mind set, which economists call self preservation, is what actually triggers the downward spiral of deflation.

From my book, *"We must not forget that a large number of businesses are linked to the housing industry. Consider, for a moment, all the different trades that play a role in the building of a home. There must be more than 100 types of businesses that get involved in some way. Working for all those businesses are millions of people who will lose their jobs very quickly when the bubble bursts. Even now, the refinance fountain is slowing down due to higher interest rates. Millions of Americans are living paycheck to paycheck. If we stop spending, companies will have to cut expenses by slashing wages or laying people off, or both."* This is the downward cycle that the Federal Reserve is most concerned with. Deflation is very foreign to us. The last time it occurred was during the Great Depression. And it lasted only a few years. It always requires a pre-existing and over-extended credit bubble, and a government that tries too hard to control it. It always ends in disaster. It is twice as bad as stagflation. Indeed, it was deflation that was behind the depression of the 1930s, while stagflation was behind the recession of the 1970s.

The flip side to the deflation argument is the fact that the United States is not the only country demanding oil. China and India have developed an insatiable thirst for the black gold as well. That said, if these countries' economies continue to grow without relying on America to supply their jobs and the products we Americans desire, worldwide inflation fueled by soaring demand for oil may emerge as the paramount problem. But if these countries slip back to the way they did things twenty years ago and the world takes on the idea of protectionism, we will see a worldwide deflation.

In terms of hyper-inflation, which the United States has never had to endure, we have to look at what happened to Germany in the early twenties. The German currency was devalued so badly that it took a wheel barrel full of money to purchase a simple loaf of bread. If something like this happens again, gold prices will shoot through the roof—possibly to as high as $20,000 per ounce, if not higher. However, with what appears to be a topping out of the commodities, Americans will have to deal with deflation. Cash will be king once again.

The causes of the Greatest Depression of all time are quite clear and disturbing. The decisions our leaders make over the next few years will determine the fate of this country. Many will wonder if America will survive this time, just as our fathers wondered in the 1780s, 1860s and the 1930s.

Chapter 4

The Darkest Winter

Winters in Iowa can be mild, with only a little snow. Or they can be stormy and bitterly cold, sparing no one from their icy fury. I remember that working on the farm in winter was extremely difficult. Even getting out of bed was a struggle, as my family lived in a house with two wood-burning stoves and no running water.

To keep warm at night, we slept between a pair of flannel sheets with three or four blankets. When we woke up and rolled out of bed, our feet would feel like icicles as we touched down on the nearly frozen floor and scampered downstairs. We made a beeline for the stoves, warming our front sides first and forcing our backs to wait their turn to thaw out. Then we'd switch sides. The moment we did, our front sides would start to freeze again.

I never did like the cold, and that is one reason I don't live in Iowa anymore. Just thinking about those nights and days when temperatures stayed below zero gives me the chills.

Surviving those frosty Midwest winters required toughness and the ability to endure adversity. Those same qualities will prove to be crucial for all Americans in the coming years as the country plunges headlong toward an economic winter: the next great depression. It unfortunately—and undoubtedly—will be the worst economic crisis of all time.

The seven to twenty years of despair that are about to wash over this nation like a tsunami will not be mild and will affect every man, woman and child. Almost every American will be affected by the crash of the stock and housing markets, which will trigger the loss of millions of jobs. As the voices of the late 1990s cried, "Prosperity for everyone," soon new voices will cry, "Hardship for everyone." As the forces of deflation, not inflation, tighten their icy grip on the United States, a dark economic winter will arrive.

The Great Depression of the Thirties

To catch a glimpse of the next depression, we need to revisit the last one. Numerous books have been written about that devastating economic disaster—what started it, the people who endured it and why recovery came so slowly.

What's amazing is that three-quarters of a century later, economists and historians are still debating what caused the historic stock market crash of 1929 and the Great Depression of the 1930s, and whether those events were connected.

Some scholars actually believe there was no connection between the crash and the hard times that followed. It's never a good sign when some of the smartest people in the world can't figure that out. Unfortunately, we are destined to repeat history precisely because those who should know are clueless about an event that dramatically changed this country and was so defining that it closed out one era and started another!

The Calm before the Storm

In the book, *Rainbow's End: The Crash of 1929*, author Maury Klein wrote about several individuals who helped shape the crash and depression. One was President Herbert Hoover, who was fingered more than anyone else for the hard times. Another was Benjamin Strong, who, as governor of the New York Federal Reserve Bank, became the most influential member of the Federal Reserve System.

Klein shines a different light on Hoover, providing us insight into the former president's views regarding the stock market in the mid-1920s. "Unlike many priests of the New Era, however, Hoover did not bask in the glow of the steadily rising stock market," Klein wrote. "He had long opposed what he called the 'growing tide of speculation' and as early as 1925 had urged Adolph Miller of the Federal Reserve Board to restrict credit. Three times in 1926, beginning on

New Year's Day, Hoover warned against 'real estate and stock speculation and its possible extension into commodities with inevitable inflation, the overextension of installment buying' and similar perils. 'Psychology plays a large part in the business movements,' he added, 'and optimism can only land us on the shores of depression.'"[1] Little did Hoover know his own words would come back to haunt him four years later.

As the economy continued to expand in 1928, Hoover changed his mind and declared during his campaign for the Republican Party's nomination that America was headed for even more prosperity. Nothing advanced the notion more that the nation was headed for good times than Hoover's acceptance speech later that year. In that address, he stated, "We in America today are nearer to the final triumph over poverty than ever before in the history of any land. The poorhouse is vanishing from among us. We have not yet reached the goal, but given a chance to go forward with the policies of the last eight years, and we shall soon, with the help of God, be in sight of the day when poverty will be banished from this nation."[2]

As we all know, it didn't turn out that way. Instead of more good times, a depression got underway in mid-1930 and it persisted through 1937. It delivered seven-plus years of poverty for several million Americans, as more than 13 million of the 52 million available workers were jobless. Twenty five percent of Americans were unemployed. And it left Hoover with anything but a flattering legacy. Perhaps the power that comes with being the President of the United States blinded him of what he believed and spoke about just a few years before. He was in the wrong place at the wrong time. And as people repeat history, President Bush may inherit a similar legacy.

As for Strong, he actually died before the depression in October 1928. However, just before his death, Strong sounded alarm bells. He wasn't concerned so much about the "easy money" policy, but he was worried about the nation's prevailing attitude. "I do not think the problem is necessarily one of security prices or of available volume of credit, or even of discount rates," Strong wrote in one of his letters. "It is really a problem of psychology. The country's state of mind has been highly speculative, advancing prices have been based upon a realization of wealth and prosperity; ...speculative tendencies are all the more difficult to deal with...The problem now is so to shape our policy as to avoid a calamitous break in the stock market, a panicky feeling about money, a setback to business because of the change in psychology."[3]

This same state of mind is the key to our future. With the rising stock market prices and the paper wealth of homeowners from 2003–2007, we have kept this negative psychology at bay for now. The more talk we hear about a New Era or New Economy, and booms without crashes, the more people will be willing to take risks. The more investors who believe the Dow Jones will just keep on climbing to, say 36,000 or higher, the more people will invest. The "realization of wealth and prosperity" gave increasingly more people the opportunity to speculate in the stock market and real estate. And as a result, expectations are extremely high now. The early part of 2008 may have begun a time, however, when investors stopped buying stocks and started selling them in earnest. From 2005 to 2007, we were at a period in history called the calm before the storm. We are talking about a period when the weather is sunny and warm, and there appears to be no threat of a storm, and yet a killer hurricane is only hours away.

The summer of 1929 was just such a time of sunny and warm days, when it came to both the weather and economy. The economy was purring along like a well-oiled engine with no breakdown in sight. The high-flying automobile industry, for example, was doing particularly well.

In the book *The Hungry Years*, author T. H. Watkins wrote, "Ford was hardly free of competitors. There were forty-four other automobile-makers in business by 1929, although the big three of Ford, General Motors and Chrysler were responsible for the manufacture and sale of more than 80 percent of the nearly 4.5 million cars built in the United States every year."[4] In August, times were so good, as Klein wrote, that "Henry Ford watched Model A number 2,000,000 roll off the assembly line less than seven months after number 1,000,000 had made its debut."[5]

The automobile wasn't the only hot item in 1929. Sales of radio and home appliances set records throughout the late Twenties. In the book, *The Great Depression*, Robert S. McElvaine wrote, "Productivity increased astronomically. Between 1920 and 1929, output per person-hour soared upward by 63 percent. If the economy was to stay afloat, someone had to buy these products. Many of them were new. Starting from a tiny base in 1922, sales of radios had increased by 1,400 percent by 1929. There was a similar, if not quite so spectacular, explosion in sales of such household appliances as vacuum cleaners, electric irons, refrigerators and washing machines. Such new industries helped greatly in producing the economic boom of the decade."[6]

But even though the economy looked good on the outside, its continued health depended on two critical fundamentals: public confidence and continued spending by the well-to-do. Were either one of these to falter, the economy would slip. Yet industries continued to increase production because everyone thought the economy would just keep on expanding. Business people were convinced that 1930 would turn out to be yet another banner year.

However, the crash of the stock market started a downward spiral in the American psyche and the nation was never the same after that. America's confidence was shattered. Because of this, Americans started to cut back on their spending to pay off debt. But by then it was too late. The calm before the storm had given way to a category 5 killer economic hurricane.

The Crash of 1929

They call it Black Tuesday. That's because the worst stock market crash in U.S. history fell on a Tuesday: October 29, 1929. Billions of dollars were lost. Millions of lives were ruined. Panic and fear seized investors as 16,410,030 shares changed hands on that historic day. That was even more than the stunning 12,900,000 shares that changed hands just a few days before, on October 24, which came to be known as Black Thursday. Both were the type of days no one forgets. They were stamped forever in people's minds. Most remembered exactly what they were doing, where they were, and what time it was when they heard the shocking and sobering news.

But what caused the stock market to crumble? It was probably the unseen change in psychology. Most investors saw the sluggish activity the month before as a normal correction to the then-all-time closing high of 381.10 recorded on Sept. 3. Also, during the first part of October volume increased to the downside. Signs that something was very wrong should have become obvious on Oct. 21. The Dow declined to 314.55 intraday. That represented a plunge of more than 17 percent from the record high. And it came with the highest volume— 6,090,000 shares—that had been recorded since March 26 of that year. Furthermore, this fall to 314.55 was less than 10 points short of a 20 percent decline, something most economists today define as a bear market.

On Oct. 23, the Dow seemed to stabilize. It peaked at 329.94, some 9 points above the closing on the 21st. However, in her book *Six Days in October: The Stock Market Crash of 1929*, Karen Blumenthal wrote, "in the last hours of trading stock prices seemed to melt. Out of nowhere, every one dropped a shocking $5 or $15 a share in frantic trading because no one would step up to buy them. More than 2.6 million shares changed hands in the chaotic final hour of trading, as many as might trade in a regular day. When the gong that ended trading rang at 3 p.m., the market was weak and trembling."[7] The intra-day low of 303.84 and the closing at 305.85 could have been the reason for the sell-off in the last hour, as it represented a decline of exactly 20 percent from the record high and confirmed the arrival of a bear market.

Unfortunately, that last hour was just the beginning of panic at the New York Stock Exchange. On Oct. 24, panic selling continued. "Within minutes, prices started to sink, weighted down by a powerful, unseen force. The price declines were eye-popping. General Electric's price slid $25 a share; Westinghouse was down $20, General Motors fell more than $12. The shares of Auburn Auto, another car maker, had dropped $77 a share on Wednesday. On Thursday, it plunged another $70, to $190. Millions of shares were changing hands as small and large investors tried to preserve something of their winnings and get out. With each drop in price, someone was losing money."[8]

If some wealthy bankers hadn't decided to buy millions of dollars in shares in a last-ditch bid to shore up the market, the carnage would have been worse. After notching an intra-day low of 272.32, the Dow actually closed at 299.47, only 5 points off the previous day's close. But the damage had been done. Investors had lost a combined $3 billion.

Bankers wanted President Hoover to issue a statement to try to calm investors and assure the American public that the stock market was stable.

But this didn't sit well with Hoover, who in private might have wanted to say, "I told you so," to each and every banker in the country. After all, he had battled Wall Street during the first year of his term. He had tried to slow down the over-speculation that had come to possess the market.

As Blumenthal put it, "To President Hoover, it was an 'orgy of speculation.' Stock prices were too high, he was sure, and the painful declines of October 23 and October 24 were long overdue. Even if he believed this with all his heart, however, on October 25, he had to come up with something more cheerful and reassuring to say publicly to the American people. The president settled on a statement that had all the spice of a bowl of oatmeal: 'The fundamental business of the country, that is production and distribution of commodities, is on a sound and prosperous basis.' The president noted that production and consumption were still at high levels, worker wages and productivity were increasing, and other factors looked good."[9] The president's statement seemed to put the brakes on selling. The Dow added almost 2 points to close at 301.22 on Friday the 25th. Saturday's half day delivered more of the same, as the Dow closed at 298.97.

Then came Monday: It turned out to be yet another highly volatile day, as the Dow lost 38 points and closed at 260. The bear market was beginning to awaken. And like a bear that has been away for a long winter's nap, this market was ready for the next kill. The big kill, of course, arrived the following day on what we all know from our history books as Black Tuesday—the worst one-day loss up to that time.

In the book, *Black Tuesday: The Stock Market Crash of 1929*, author Barbara Silberdick Feinherg wrote, "At 10:30 A.M., 650,000 shares of U.S. Steel had been dumped on the market and the stock's price per share plummeted from $205 to $179. During the first six minutes of trading, General Electric stock dropped a dollar every 10 seconds. Westinghouse lost two dollars a minute during the first quarter of an hour... By eleven o'clock, the stocks were being sold for whatever price they could bring... The wave of selling spread quickly. Shareholders all over the United States had flocked to their brokers and watched in disbelief as the tumbling stock prices were posted on chalkboards. The value of their shares continued to drop so they decided to cut their losses."[10] To make things worse, bankers were unwilling to step in to prop up the market.

The day's ending numbers were unbelievable and downright horrific. A record 16,410,000 shares had changed hands. Fourteen billion dollars of stock value had vanished into thin air. In less than 60 days, the Dow Jones had lost more than 40 percent of its overall worth. Gone were the savings of tens of thousands of investors. Gone also was a prosperous future.

Investors, brokers, and bankers were all big losers. Investors lost personal savings and had no way of paying off debts, due to the fact they had bought most of their stocks on margin. Brokers wound up with fewer clients and most went out of business because no one was left to satisfy bankers. It was those same bankers, of course, who had lent anywhere from 50 percent to 90 percent of their deposits to investors to buy stocks on margin. But because there was little cash to go around, millions of dollars in bank loans went unpaid. Without a doubt, margin was one of the key reasons for the Crash of 1929. And that crash was the primary trigger for the Great Depression.

The Great Depression 1930–1937

Following the crash, most Americans were in shock over the magnitude of money that had disappeared. Comedians, who had invested in the market, had no choice but to make fun of how much they had lost trading stocks. Suddenly, the Roaring Twenties seemed like a majestic, make-believe land far, far away, that would never be inhabited again. If any good were to come out of the crash, it would be the death of the foolishness and individualism the Roaring Twenties had given birth to. America was about to see what it was really made of. The world would soon find out whether the nation would run and hide from its problems or work hard despite them, knowing better days would eventually return.

Unfortunately, the attitude of run and hide lingered for the first two or three years of the depression. Times had to get worse before they could get better. Most Americans had no place to turn. The government had not planned for a depression and had no way of stopping it once it started. There were no government programs, such as unemployment insurance or welfare, for the needy to fall back on.

But as bad as things were, leaders tried to comfort the nation with the thought that the crisis would be short-lived. And there were signs early on that they might be right. By the spring of 1930, the Dow Jones had rebounded from a low of 198.69 on Nov. 13, 1929, to a high of 293.43 on April 12—a 48 percent jump. President Hoover seized on this trend as an indication that the worst was over. "We have now passed the worst and with continued unity of effort shall rapidly recover,"[11] Hoover told the country.

However, the bounce turned out to be nothing more than a bear market rally. Investors who thought they could win back losses became losers once again in another price free-fall during the summer and autumn. This final collapse was the last straw for the struggling economy, as production decreased each and every month that year.

American's middle class, after flourishing during the 1920s, was on the brink of vanishing as early as 1931. Millions were left homeless, with no hope of regaining the prosperity they had enjoyed a few years earlier. "The feeling of helplessness was a caul whose weight could bring the strongest man down in tears, as a boy discovered when he came upon his father in the empty coal bin of the family's house in Brookline, Massachusetts. The father was crying."[12] "We had owned a small bakery that had failed a few months before," the boy recalled. "Things would get worse for us later on, and for a couple years we were in really bad shape, but to me the low point of the depression will always be the sight of my father that day, crying in the coal bin."[13]

Similar stories abounded, as dreams turned into real-life nightmares. In New York City, during the "night, some 3,300 street people, including as many as 100 women, found sleep on the beds, benches and floors of the six-story Municipal Lodging House on East Twenty-fifth Street. Thousands more clustered wherever they could in what would come to be called 'Hoovervilles,' in bitter mockery of the president, shantytowns constructed of everything that came to hand, from packing crates to hundreds of tin cans flattened out and nailed to boards. This was just the beginning of a long period of great suffering for many Americans."[14]

"Drifters," who literally did not own anything but the clothes on their back, crisscrossed America in search of work. Farmers were especially hard hit. Many lost farms to bankers, or to buyers who bought them out for pennies on the dollar. Prices had fallen so much they couldn't make a profit selling their crops.

A 1932 event in Chicago came to define just how far American had fallen. In the book *Since Yesterday*, author Frederick Lewis Allen wrote about an American woman who said, "One vivid, gruesome moment of those dark days we shall never forget. We saw a crowd of some 50 men fighting over a barrel of garbage, which had been set outside the back door of a restaurant. American citizens fighting for scraps of food like animals."[15]

In that same year, on July 8, the Dow Jones index hit a bottom of 41.22, an eighty-nine percent drop from the high in September 1929. Ultimately, it would take more than five years under Franklin D. Roosevelt for America to pull itself up by the bootstraps. Of course, by the time America did put itself back on a path to a more prosperous future, yet another crisis was lurking around the corner. President Roosevelt would a short time later address a joint session of Congress and announce that, "yesterday, Dec. 7, 1941—a date which will live in infamy—the United States was suddenly and deliberately attacked." And World War II would deliver still more hard times for the nation.

Who will be responsible for the coming depression?

People in general, and especially Americans, tend to have short memories. Besides that, we tend to be arrogant. In large part, that is why America is headed for another depression.

President Bush, who is currently telling us everything looks rosy, is leading us down a road of no return. And even as the economy transitions from a mild downturn to a recession to a severe depression, our current leaders—in their arrogance—will blame everything and everyone but themselves. President Bush will refuse to admit he and his administration bankrupted America. He may blame Congress. He may blame the current Federal Reserve Chairman Bernanke. He may even try to pin responsibility for the looming disaster on Alan Greenspan. In fact, just weeks before finishing this book, Bush, believing all cameras were off claimed Wall Street was drunk as it dealt in "fancy financial instruments." Once again, Bush will never take personal responsibility for helping create the largest credit and real estate bubble in the history of the United States. My hope, though, is that he will prove me wrong and at some point level with the nation—even if he waits until after he leaves office to do so.

The irreversible damage to the economy began when President Bush and the Federal Reserve artificially halted a normal business cycle and left us with a mini-recession in early 2001. Bush likes to remind people that he stopped a possible major recession in its tracks. He and the Fed did that by slashing interest rates to their lowest level in 40 years. The low rates provided cheap money for a huge number of Americans.

However, Al Friedberg of Welling@Weeden.com stated on March 23, 2001, that the extraordinarily low interest rates were not what America needed and in fact led to other problems. "Resources have been mis-allocated because of the cheapness of the credit in both stock and credit markets," Friedberg stated, "so, you're not going to solve the problem by making money cheaper again."[16] Furthermore, whatever economic expansion we've had since 2003 has come from more and more debt, not savings. Another way to look at this is the comparison to baseball's illegal use of steroids. All those that used the illegal drug are frauds and cheaters. They don't deserve to be called baseball players. The economic expansion we've had since 2003 is the same. It is not real.

Therefore, the inevitable correction to this

credit bubble will be very painful. It's too bad we didn't learn from history and forgot the insight Gotfried Haberler provided for us in 1937. In his book *Prosperity and Depression*, Haberler wrote: "The length and severity of depressions depend partly on the magnitude of the 'real' maladjustments which developed during the preceding boom, and partly on the aggravating monetary and credit conditions."[17]

In May of 2005, President Bush had his work cut out for him. The last thing Bush wanted, of course, was for the artificially inflated stock market bubble, housing bubble, and credit bubble to start busting on his watch. But by the beginning of 2008 these bubbles started to burst. In an attempt stop or at the least slow the bursting, President Bush and Congress passed an economic stimulus package, something that was essentially a continuation of Bush's easy money policy. Along with the Federal Reserve, President Bush is hoping his economic cures will keep at bay the painful and inevitable corrections that began to take place in his last year as president. What's puzzling is why we didn't hear a senator or U.S. representative question why we needed the stimulus package and the rate cuts in the first place. Mr. Bush needs to understand that just as he took credit for a strong economy when blue skies prevailed, he also needs to take the blame for the dark storm clouds on the horizon. Give the president his due; he has done a great job keeping the general population confident in the system. However, the damage has already been done and there is no turning back. And the public's confidence is now shaken.

It's amazing that our government leaders believe that they can fix the credit crunch by adding still more and more debt. They just don't get it. You can't put a fire out when you keep putting wood on it.

Indeed, when it's all said and done, Bush could and should be remembered as the worst president in U.S. history. His approval rating at the start of his second term was the lowest since that of the late President Richard Nixon, who was forced to resign in his second term because of the Watergate scandal. Furthermore, we still do not know how the Iraq War (many would say Bush's War) will end. Unfortunately, the next President will inherit a large number of problems created by the Bush administration.

His most disgraceful legacy, however, may actually be the towns that will bear his name. As communities continue to lose homes to foreclosures, these ghost towns may become known as "Bushtowns". Also, remember those unflattering Hoovervilles? When economic conditions worsen, look for hundreds of cities to fill with the ranks of unemployed people, and for these frustrated Americans who live in them to dub their communities "Bushtowns" as well. They will point their fingers right at Bush and the Republican Party. Bush may very well replace Hoover in future history books as the President who started the Greatest Depression of all time and did the most damage to the economy of any President in the history of the United States. It will be much worse for Mr. Bush and his party if Sen. John McCain of Arizona wins the 2008 presidential election. If McCain wins, the Republican Party may not have another president for at least twenty years. The party may even be terminated.

Currently, Bush, the two-term GOP president has no choice but to continue to insist the economy is purring along just fine when, in fact, it is on the verge of collapse.

As the 2008 elections approaches, Sen. Barack Obama the Democratic nominee for president will need to face the fact that there is a historic economic crisis on the horizon. Sen. Obama will need to convince Americans the real reason they are losing their jobs is Bush and the Republican Party.

If America selects Obama as our new president, we will be patient with him for a time. But the honeymoon won't last long. Obama will have about 2 years to turn the nation around. If he is not successful, the nation will turn on him. We Americans will be seeking the truth no matter how bad the news is. And we will be more than ready to place the blame on someone. Ultimately, the blame must be placed on George W. Bush, his administration and his party. However, the approaching bear market, which will be the worst in history, will not care who is in office.

The Abyss

This year—2008—will be a critical one not just for the presidency, but for the stock market and the economy as well. Millions of Americans have never experienced anything like what is coming. In the 51 years I have lived, I vaguely remember the 1973 fuel shortage, the 1987 stock market crash, and the early 1990s coastal real estate collapse. But most have never seen a bear market like the one that devoured investors in 1929. If America thought the first leg down in today's bear market was bad (Dow Jones 7,181 October 2002), the next leg will crush them. Those that should know will not know what hit them. Most will have no clue what happened. Maybe their first thought will be, "Isn't this supposed to happen to our children or our children's children? Why now? Why me?"

American's psychology, will determine the precise start of the depression. In the book *The Fourth Turning,* authors William Strauss and Neil

Howe actually predicted that one of the catalysts to start the crisis could be a global terrorist group blowing up an aircraft. And certainly, 9/11 was a wake-up call. However, nothing really changed. Culture wars still rage. America remains divided. Its spend-until-you-drop philosophy and the-one-with-the-most-toys-wins mentality are not going to change without another, very severe, wake-up call. A stock market crash is the most probable call.

And it doesn't help that government officials and economists are still so focused on inflation that they have set themselves up to be blindsided by the downward spiral of deflation. If the Dow Jones cannot stay above 10,000, which many believe to be a critical psychological level for the markets, we will see a crash not seen since 1929. Once the Dow matches its October 10, 2002, low of 7181, we will have reached the point of no return. The amount of money that will be lost in the next leg down will be nothing short of staggering. This time not billions, but rather trillions of dollars will vanish. When the Dow Jones index falls below the point of no return, the worst depression in history will be upon us.

As 2009 approaches, consumers will be forced to cut back on spending even more. Deflation will rear its ugly head as debt-conscious consumers pay bills and shop for deals. Price wars and competition will heat up. Companies will do whatever they can to maintain their market shares.

All this will cause the economy to contract and businesses to lay people off.

Most industries will be affected, but none worse than home building. In the years following 1998, builders convinced the robust economy would crank forever, built millions of new houses throughout the country. According to the U.S. Commerce Department the nation saw a record $998 billion pumped into construction of various types in 2004. New-home construction increased by a stunning 14 percent from the year before and a record $543 billion was spent on building houses alone. But by 2009, many of these homes will be empty, as over-capacity becomes the standard for more than a decade. Indeed, many already were becoming empty in 2008 as a result of the worst wave of foreclosures this country has ever seen. In his book, Business Cycles and National Income, Alvin H. Hansen, as he called the drop in construction in 1928 "catastrophic" wrote, "No explanation of the boom of the twenties or the severity and duration of the depression of the thirties is adequate which leaves out of account the great expansion and contraction in building activity".[18]

Come 2009–2010, the majority of Americans will deny the existence of a depression—that is until they themselves are standing in line with their neighbors, waiting to withdraw their hard-earned savings. Unfortunately, only the first ones in line will receive any money. "Bank runs" a la 1929 could occur in every state. Thousands of banks will close their doors and claim bankruptcy.

As I have been saying, a depression is imminent. It is not a question of if, but when. That said, no one knows the timing. Even as I write this new book I have to admit that timing something like a depression within 3—5 years is extremely hard. Furthermore, the coming historic crisis will hinge largely on what initially causes the credit bubble to pop. This bubble appears to have started bursting in August 2007.

But how severe will this depression be? There are three potential scenarios: The first is a depression milder than the 1930s variety. The second scenario is a depression worse than the Great Depression, but marked by recovery several years later. The third is a massive depression that leads to a total collapse of the economy and destroys the middle class, leaving only the very rich and very poor. This scenario could prove so destructive it could trigger the dividing up of the United States into several different countries, not unlike the way the old Soviet Union was carved up after the fall of communism. Obviously, the first scenario would be the least damaging.

But a more severe scenario is likely because the approaching winter will unleash an unrelenting toll on American's middle class. At no time in history has the middle class been so prosperous—and yet so vulnerable. In order for most middle-class families to sustain their standard of living, both parents must work. If just one of them loses his or her job, those parents' ability to pay their bills and provide for their families becomes extremely difficult. And, so, with the coming depression, families with a mortgage, credit card debt, and car loans will be forced to cut back drastically or risk losing everything they worked for. Many will find themselves living with relatives or, worse, homeless. Millions will find it impossible to provide for bare necessities.

Some even will have to beg for food and clothes. Children will have trouble staying in school—not because of bad grades but because their parents won't have the money to pay for their education and clothing. Teens will have no choice but to mature quickly and take on responsibility to help their families survive. Americans will truly feel that they have fallen into the abyss, a bottomless chasm impossible to climb out of.

Most Americans have seen only good economic times or mildly difficult times. We have been given whatever our hearts have desired. We have done everything under the sun. America has enjoyed the world's highest standard of living for more than 60 years. Because of our prosperity, the vast majority of us won't even entertain the thought that America is destined for a horrific fall from grace. But people said similar things about the "unsinkable" *Titanic*. The approaching winter will be a long, cold, and bitter one. For millions of Americans, it will deliver the worst conditions they have ever lived through. And those conditions will trigger a shift from trying to collect the most toys to trying to survive. Just making it one more day will become a monumental task.

Chapter 5

Will America Survive This Time?

It will take a fair amount of time for the majority of Americans to finally realize—and accept—the fact that America has slipped into a depression. It will not be a pleasant reality. Once we do, many we be in a state of shock and not know what to do. It's at this time most Americans will question the nation's survival. Just has one must change their mind set to recover from one's own personal depression; it will require Americans to do the same. Personal sacrifice, teamwork, and patience for what will seem like an eternity will be required if we are to return to normalcy. We will have to first forgive the very people that helped start this approaching depression: government leaders such as President Bush, for bankrupting America, and Federal Reserve Chairman Alan Greenspan, for encouraging the largest credit bubble in history to be formed. Americans also will have to forgive themselves for living beyond their means, blindly believing government leaders and failing to plan and save in a prudent manner for their families and future.

Who Will Lead Us?

Once again, if America is going to recover from this mother of all depressions reasonably quickly, we are going to have to find a leader with the character of an Abraham Lincoln, the president who led the United States to victory in the Civil War and helped to abolish slavery. We will need a leader like Franklin D. Roosevelt, whose great determination and vision led the nation back up from the Great Depression. America will need a leader who is neither extreme right nor extreme left. The depth of the unprecedented crisis will require a leader who is more concerned about helping the poor and homeless than winning a second term. Illinois Sen. Barack Obama may be that man.

As well, we will need a leader who will not lie, if that, of course, is even possible. We will need a leader with the courage to challenge the rich to do their part, to contribute to charity the same percentage they gave during the boom years. America will need a leader who has a genuine humility, someone who doesn't just say "God bless America" because it sounds good, but because they truly rely on the Creator rather than himself.

For the sake of our international security, we will need someone who can address head on and fix the very serious problems Bush has created abroad. It is obvious that the number of countries with a dislike for the United States has multiplied since he took office. True, President Bush's quest for a worldwide democracy may indeed be commendable. The freedoms we have enjoyed for nearly 230 years are the envy of the world. And most of us would love to see a world without dictators. But at the same time, many have the conviction that "bullying" world leaders into running their governments the way the United States does is flat-out wrong. These Americans would more than likely agree with an old quote from cowboy comedian Will Rogers, who said, "If there is one thing that we do worse than any other nation, it is try and manage somebody else's affairs."

Furthermore, some Americans realize that the example we have set in running up record government and consumer debt is all that many world leaders need to say no to democracy. It is a shame that our leaders have made the United States the largest debtor country in the world. And all that talk about freedom? What freedom do we really have, when we owe so much debt? America, we need perhaps most of all a leader who will humble out and admit that those who have directed our affairs these last seven plus years have been arrogant, prideful, and more concerned about pursuing their own interests than those of the country as a whole. And that leader will have to humbly go to our creditors—foreign nations—and ask them to forgive our debt.

Meanwhile, let us pray that one of the bold declarations in President Bush's second inaugural address doesn't come back to haunt us, just as a statement by former President Hoover did some 80 years ago. Bush, you'll remember, declared, "It is the policy of the United States to seek and support the growth of democratic movements and institutions in every nation and culture, with the ultimate goal of ending tyranny." Hoover had a different goal, but one that was every bit as lofty and sweeping in scope. "We have not yet reached the goal," Hoover said. "But we shall soon, with the help of God, be in sight of the day when poverty shall be banished from this nation." We all know what happened to Hoover's goal; instead of ushering in an era where only prosperous people walked the streets of America, it gave way to the Great Depression—and record poverty levels. We can only shudder at the thought of where Bush's goal may actually lead.

We Are Our Brother's Keeper

By the end of the economic winter, more than 30 percent of Americans will have lost their jobs. Many of them will be homeless and have no choice but to beg for basic necessities, things we all take for granted today. Because the majority of us—the herd—will err on the pessimistic side during these years, Americans will sense the need to be protective and cautious. The rich and those who keep their jobs will be tempted to be uncaring and look down on those with nothing but the shirts on their backs. Yet it will be incumbent on the rich to help rescue the country by uniting to feed, clothe, and shelter the poor. Large cities throughout the country are going to have to organize and supply numerous soup kitchens in order to feed the masses that will have become poor overnight.

We must avoid, at all cost, a situation like that which occurred in the Great Depression, where millions of acres of crops were destroyed because of the deflated prices. Farmers, in order to save money and avoid a greater loss, decided to plow under their crops. As well, livestock in the millions were destroyed as part of a last-ditch strategy to halt the free-fall of prices that had been brought about by overproduction. All this led to one of the most shocking ironies of the Great Depression: Millions went without food and clothing even as surplus of those commodities were destroyed—the very supplies that could have done so much good.

During this rapidly approaching depression of all time those of us who can do something to help must do so. Americans must unify and help those who will be beaten down by the kind of severe trials most of us are unfamiliar with. If the rich, and those who manage to keep their jobs, want to sustain their way of life, they will have to pool their resources and help save America. In 1930, it was often heard on the streets of America: "Brother, can you spare me a dime?" Look for something similar to be spoken as this first major depression of the new millennium takes hold—with an adjustment, of course, to reflect today's values. Don't be surprised if you hear someone say, "Brother, can you spare me a dollar?" And we must not turn a deaf ear. We all must give our fellow Americans something to hope for.

America, We Have Recovered Before

After every crisis, dating back to the day we won our independence, we have always found a way to snap back. In 1781, after we sent the Brits back where they came from, defeated and shamed, we were free. Free from British law. Free from British taxes. It was a time our forefathers never forgot because it was the glorious birth of a great nation.

In 1860, the United States did not want war, but it happened anyway. The Civil War was the bloodiest ever to occur on American soil. More than 600,000 Americans died. During this horrific crisis, America was on the verge of destroying itself. And the recovery from that crisis was excruciatingly slow and painful. Still, it happened. America found a way to bounce back with resilience.

And, of course, there was 1930, the advent of the worst depression in history until now. After America depleted its excesses and overcapacities, which corrected the imbalances, the country was on its way back up. Then we became involved with World War II and more hard times, which postponed the long-anticipated recovery for even longer. But after the war, Americans would enjoy prosperity like never before. American recovered once again and became one of the most popular countries in the world. Everyone wanted to come here to live.

But will America survive this time? Perhaps every American will ask that question at some point during the next several years. As those hardy Americans of the Great Depression fell on their knees in the 1930s and '40s, we will once again fall to our knees and ask God for deliverance.

Chapter 6

What Can Americans Do?

What you can do now depends on when you read this book. As I write this chapter, 75 percent of Americans believe the United States is already in a recession. President Bush, on the other hand, is still claiming we're only experiencing a slowdown in the economy and that our financial institutions are strong and resilient. On July 15, 2008 during a White House news conference Mr. Bush said, "The bottom line is this. We're going through a tough time. But our economy's continued growing, consumers are spending, businesses are investing, exports continue increasing and American productivity remains strong. We can have confidence in the long-term foundation of our economy and I believe we will come through this challenge stronger than ever before." He's hoping the economy will stay above water until he leaves. He does admit these are "challenging times," but his ultimate goal is to convince us that his tax rebates and economic stimulus package will help us turn the corner toward a better economy by the fall of 2008. Sounds like Republican President Hoover, who maintained the economy was improving back in March of 1930, only to see the greatest depression of that time begin just a few months later.

So what can you do to protect yourself, your family and friends from the crisis that's fast approaching? This may have been the primary reason you purchased this book. Most people will not know what to do. Answers will not come easy and may not come at all. No one has all the answers. From **The Approaching Winter**, my predictions of a stock market crash before 2008 and the topping of oil and gold prices were incorrect. Even though my hunch that the housing and credit bubbles would burst was correct, this book still will fall short of having *all* the right answers. Authors of books similar to this one ask the question, "What if?" We work in the realm of probabilities. None of us has a crystal ball.

Still, there is a high *probability* that an economic depression will occur. And your chances of surviving it will be high if you are quick to respond to the information that follows. Timing will be extremely important.

Make Relationships That Will Last

Over the last 20 years, individualism has become the norm and is partly to blame for the unraveling now occurring. Now is the time to cultivate relationships that will help you and your family survive the approaching winter. No one really knows how deep the coming depression will be. However, with today's larger world population, the probability of intense hardship for many people is high.

Now is the time to start reaching out to your immediate family and to your friends at church and/or work. In their book, The Fourth Turning, Strauss and Howe wrote, "When the Fourth Turning arrives, your family will become your ultimate safety net. Maintain relationships of trust with your extended family, from grandparents to grandchildren, in-laws to distant cousins. As other supports weaken, your household will function best if it is multi-generational, with young and old caring for each other's special needs....The Fourth Turning will not be a good time to be, or feel, socially stranded." It is also equally important to have friends of the fire and police departments. It would be a good idea to start supporting your local departments, especially if they're participating in fundraisers. Again, to the wisdom of Strauss and Howe, "Face-to-face contacts with everyone (neighbors, bosses, employees, customers, suppliers, creditors, debtors, public officials, police) will become newly important."

As you work on relationships, don't be surprised if you are the one who's actually helping others. Also, many parents will need their teenagers to help support the family. Young people will need to explore how to bring people together to fund and organize local help groups for their own families, the elderly and the poor. Teamwork will be natural for these young people. They will clearly see the selfishness and individualism of the baby boomers and won't want anything to do with it. But their hardest obstacle will be to get the rich, namely the same baby boomers, to help fund their truly beneficial tasks. I don't want to discourage these teenagers and 20-year-olds in their commendable pursuits, but they should take this warning to heart: "Scrooge" will be an appropriate label for many of the rich. Self preservation will motivate many of the well-to-do to do whatever they can to keep what they have.

Personal Debt Must be Dealt With

There is bad debt and good debt. A 30-year mortgage with a low fixed interest rate on a home that's your primary residence is good debt. But a credit card with a high balance and an interest rate of 10 percent or higher is not. And many of us have multiple credit cards that are maxed out. That is extremely unwise. We Americans are addicted to spending. Credit card companies send us three or four card offers a week, many of them with a zero percent introductory rate for the first six months or year. But if we are late on only one payment, the rate automatically rises to 24% or higher. We are bombarded by advertising on TV, radio, newspapers and magazines. Advertising, which was one of the reasons Americans unraveled during the late Twenties, will again be one of the causes of the unraveling of the first decade of the 21st Century.

But how did we become so carefree with our money and the credit we received? We followed the example of our government leaders. It is amazing that we have allowed a government that carries a negative balance of almost $10 trillion to be in control. How did we, the people, allow our government leaders, Republicans and Democrats alike, to make our nation the most indebted country of all time? And we must not deceive ourselves; all of us will pay for it. Credit equals debt. Debt equals slavery.

Now is the time to do whatever you can to get out of debt as quickly as possible. What did you do with that tax rebate President Bush sent you? Hopefully you used it to pay down debt---credit cards, a car loan or your mortgage. I'd suggest going even farther. Cut up those credit cards and, if your budget allows, start to double or triple your minimum payment on them. Start spending your money on food, clothes, shelter, transportation and school only. Get your life back and make war on your debt. In his book, *Crash*

Profits, Martin D. Weiss, Ph.D. gave his readers 10 steps to reduce debt. They are as follows:

Step 1: Declare your own personal war on debt.
Step 2: Attack your credit cards first.
Step 3: Attack your credit card statement next.
Step 4: Add up your minimum monthly payments.
Step 5: Figure out how much you can pay over and above the total of all the minimum payments
Step 6: Pay off the worst ones first!
Step 7: Consider using your savings to get out of debt
Step 8: Avoid new credit cards: Period.
Step 9: Start paying down any other personal loans you may have
Step 10: Pay down your mortgage"

If possible, start saving as much as you can now. If we go into a period of deflation, the probability of which is high, your money will go farther as prices are forced down by lower demand. Also, visit www.martinweiss.com for information on the safest banks in America. Dr. Weiss is one of the nation's leading providers of a wide range of investment information. Dr. Weiss is the editor of the financial newsletter, Safe Money Report, known for its excellent track record of picking major turns in interest rates. You can subscribe to his newsletter on his Web site. The company's aim, according to its mission statement, is to empower investors to protect their savings, build their wealth, and prosper in good times or bad.

Another Web site that's very valuable is www.russtrading.com. Mr. Nicholas Russo, Jr. is one of Wall Street's most respected stock traders and is considered an authority on trends in the marketplace. He believes we all have one last chance to reinforce our financial and personal foundations before "The Big Rollover." Mr. Russo has done several seminars and you can purchase a nine-CD set of one by visiting the above Web site.

What to invest in a Bear Market

If you decide the following information applies to you, the author and publisher are not responsible for any of your investment decisions. Please consult your broker or a financial adviser before you invest.

This segment is for investors who want to make a profit or at least break even after the carnage of the bear market. It is also for anyone who wants to hedge against a loss in the value of their real estate. Think of it as insurance for your portfolio. We all know what insurance is for. We have house and car insurance to protect us from losses. Insurance is actually a hedge which is used as leverage against a crisis.

The best investment for the length of the bear market will be Exchange Traded Funds (ETFs) that rise when an index such as the Dow Jones or the S&P drop. In other words, when the Dow Jones drops 10%, the ETF rises 10%. Some ETFs are leveraged 2 to 1, which means if an index decreases in price by 10%, this ETF will rise 20%. However, the exact opposite occurs when an index rises: The ETF will either fall one to one or two to one depending on your risk tolerance. A second type of investment is Bear Mutual Funds, which again rise or fall in the opposite direction of a pool of stocks. The advantage for ETFs is that they are traded just like individual stocks in real time. However, when you place a trade using mutual funds you're usually stuck with the closing price of the fund. Investing in these funds and ETFs will require a steadying hand due to the extreme volatility of their prices. As long as index prices are trending lower, these types of investments will work for you.

The following is a list of ETFs and mutual funds you may want to consider. Just remember that my publisher and I, the author, are not responsible for any of your investment decisions. You could lose all your money. Please consult your broker or your financial adviser before investing.

Exchange Traded Funds

Ticker — Name
DOG — Short Dow30 ProShares
Seeks daily investment results that correspond to the inverse (opposite) of the daily performance of the Dow Jones Industrial Average.

PSQ — Short QQQ ProShares
Seeks daily investment results that correspond to the inverse (opposite) of the daily performance of the NASDAQ-100 Index.

SH — Short S&P500 ProShares
Seeks daily investment results that correspond to the inverse (opposite) of the daily performance of the Dow Jones Industrial Average.

DXD — Ultra Short Dow 30 ProShares
Twice the inverse (opposite) of the daily performance of the Dow Jones Index.

QID — Ultra Short QQQ ProShares
Twice the inverse (opposite) of the daily performance of the NASDAQ 100 index.

SDS — Ultra Short S&P500 ProShares
Twice the inverse (opposite) of the daily performance of the S&P 500 Index.

SRS — Ultra Short Real Estate ProShares
Twice the inverse (opposite) of the daily performance of the Dow Jones U.S. Real Estate Index.

SKF — Ultra Short Financials ProShares
Twice the inverse (opposite) of the daily performance of the Dow Jones U.S. Financial Index.

FXP — Ultra Short FTSE/XINHUA China 25 ProShares
Twice the inverse (opposite) of the daily performance of the FTSE/XINHUA China 25 Index.

Bear Mutual Funds

Ticker — Name
RYCWX — Inverse Dow 2x Strategy (H Class)
Seeks to provide investment results that inversely correspond to 200% of the daily performance of the Dow Jones Index.

RYVNX — Inverse OTC Strategy (Investor)
Seeks to provide investment results that inversely correspond to 200% of the daily performance of the NASDAQ 100 Index.

RYTPX — Inverse S&P 500 2x Strategy (H Class)
Seeks to provide investment results that inversely correspond to 200% of the daily performance of the S&P 500 Index.

For more information on ETFs, go to proshares.com. For information on bear mutual funds and additional ETFs (RFN, REC), visit rydex.com. Both of these web sites list additional options for adding "insurance" to your portfolio. Also, as the bear market ends, you'll have the funds available to go long at extremely low prices. However, the bottom of the bear trend could be just as hard to call as the top of the bull market was. You may want to start selling your short positions in percentages, such as 33% or 25% at a time. Just remember that when investors stop predicting a bottom and everyone is claiming stocks are not a good investment and could go down even more, the bottom is getting very close. The last part of chapter 1 describes what the bottom may look like.

What about Employment?

Unfortunately, due to President Bush's administration and policies over the last several years, the fast approaching depression will set an all-time unemployment record. In the 1930s, the unemployment rate peaked at 24.9% and 13 million people were out of work. It is clear that most of today's imbalances were created during Bush's two terms and will take a number of years to unravel. Hundreds of thousands of jobs will vanish overnight. By the time the depression is over a record number of people will have lost their jobs. Many of them will be homeless. Unemployment rates could even exceed 30%. So what can you do to protect yourself from being jobless? And what jobs may be available?

About 70 percent of the labor market should still be employed. Finding a job may require additional education and a career change. If your job was recently taken away, having a job that pays less is better than not having a job at all. Unfortunately, for a large number of people, taking a lower paying job will be a great struggle and hard to accept. But what jobs could be available during the depression?

Since crime, regrettably, will multiply 5 to 10 times, companies that employ security guards and sell security systems will be great places for employment. Sales of home security systems could rise in response to the increase of crime. Customer service representatives who monitor these systems could be in great demand as well.

During the economic downturn, a large number of people will have no choice but to repair their cars and household appliances. These people will not have the funds to buy new high-end items. Employment as a mechanic or household repair person (handy man) will be in great demand.

For those who are good on the phone, customer service jobs in the debt collection industry will have an ever-increasing number of job openings for several years. Many Americans are already selling their possessions on-line to pay debt and household bills. Many more Americans will hold neighborhood yard sales just to satisfy those debt collectors who call.

Those lucky enough to keep their homes will still need to heat and cool them. Consequently, utility companies will still need technicians and representatives to serve their customers.

If you are young and can afford college, aim for a career in the health care industry. With American's boomers entering retirement, many positions in this field (doctors, nurses, and health information technicians) should be available. However, due to deflation pressures expect lower salaries.

Also, look for opportunties of discovering new energy sources that will power America and the world in the future. Getting on the ground floor of a solar energy company may enable you to survive the crisis. Bad times usually give birth to new ways of thinking and over coming.

Conclusion

The approaching economic winter will cripple America much the same way a blizzard cripples the Midwest in January. Act now to protect and provide for your family. Research more by visiting the two Web sites that were presented in this chapter.

This book was written to wake Americans up to the very real possibility, and in fact strong likelihood, that we will live through a monumental crisis like the kind that historically visits us every 75 years. You may agree that a depression is coming, or you may disagree. If you disagree, as I wrote in *The Approaching Winter*, *"you may want to ask yourself some questions. The first might be, "Who is going to pay all our debt?" Another might be, "How do I think we will avoid going through a cycle that occurs in America every 75 or 80 years?"*

And ask yourself this: "Why do most people believe that the late 1990s and the early 2000s were a repeat of the Roaring Twenties, but yet virtually no one expects the 1930s to repeat after our roaring period?" Last, but not least, ask, "When the same kind of speculation is occurring in the housing market that occurred in the stock market, what makes me so sure it won't implode just as the NASDAQ did between 2000 and 2002?"

I know I've painted a bleak picture of the future, one that is not easy to accept. It wasn't easy for me to accept, either.

Before 9/11, I did not believe a depression would, or even could happen in my lifetime. For me, it was always a problem my grandchildren would have to grapple with one day many years from now. But when I considered the evidence, it was overwhelming. After accepting the idea that an actual full-blown depression could happen, I became frightened and concerned. Then I read *The Fourth Turning* a second time. It convinced me that a depression not only could happen but that an economic crisis of historic proportions was indeed imminent.

This book was written not for the scholar, but for the average American, as that is what I am. It is straight to the point and delivered with conviction. I sincerely hope that I am wrong. But, if I am right, may God be with us and have mercy on us.

Endnotes

Chapter 1

1   Myron E. Forbes, President, Pierce Arrow Motor Car Co., January 12, 1928 www.cyberhaven.com

2   Calvin Coolidge, Dec. 4, 1928 www.gold-eagle.com

3   Paul Block, editorial, 1929 www.gold-eagle.com

4   Irving Fisher, Professor of Economics, Yale University, 1929www.quotesforall.com

5   Gold and Economic Freedom, Alan Greenspan, The Objectivist, July, 1966

6   Kevin Rayburn, a time line of the 1920s

7   President Theodore Roosevelt (1858–1919, www.brainyquote.com

8   William Strauss and Neil Howe, *The Fourth Turning*, Broadway, 1997

9   ibid

10 ibid

11 Copyright by the New York Times Agency. Reprinted with permission

Chapter 2

1   Frederick Lewis Allen, Only Yesterday, (New York, 1931), p.160.

2   Ibid., p.281

3   Charles Mackay, Extraordinary Popular Delusions and the
     Madness in Crowds, Barnes & Noble Inc., June, 1994

4   Homer Hoyt, According to Hoyt: Fifty Years of Homer Hoyt:
     1916-1966, University of Wisconsin Press, 1970

5   Robert R. Prechter, Jr. The Wave Principle of Human Social
     Behavior and The New Science of Socionomics, New
     Classics Library, 1999

Chapter 3

1   Grandfather Federal Government Debt
     Report:http//mwhodges.home.att.net/debt.htm

2   ibid

3   Bureau of the Public Debt:
     www.publicdebt.treas.gov/opd/opdpenny.htm

4   Grandfather Federal Government Debt
     Report:http//mwhodges.home.att.net/debt.htm

5   http://www.crown.org/LIBRARY/ViewArticle.aspx?
     ArticleId=762, Crown Financial Ministries

6   Alan Zibel, "Personal Bankruptcy Filings Rise 40%,"
     Washingtonpost.com, The Associated Press

7   William Branigin, Washington Post, "U.S. Consumer Debt
     Grows at Alarming Rate," January 12, 2004

8   Mark Brinker, "Credit Card Debt Statistics,"
     www.hoffmanbrinker.com/credit-card-debt-
     statistics.html

9   Alan Greenspan, before the Economic Club of New York,
     New York, March 2, 2004, www.federalreserve.gov

10   Alan Greenspan, before a credit union conference, February
     22, 2004, www.rgi.com

11   Alan Greenspan, before the America's Community Bankers,
     October 26, 2004, www.forbes.com

12   Bridgewater Associates, Westport, Connecticut, March 2004
     Report

13   Tome Kelly, STLtoday.com, "Second home purchases
     surprise real estate economists," April 13, 2005,
     www/stltoday.com

14   Kevin Duffy, Prudent Bear.com, "Honey, I shrunk the Net
     Worth," March 7, 2005

15   California Association of Realtors, April 7, 2005,
     www.car.org

16   U.S. Census Bureau, Census of Housing, Historical Census of
     Housing Tables, Home Values, *Adjusted for inflation,
     2000 dollars
www.census.gov/hhes/www/housing/census/historic/values.html

17   www.realtor.org, Walter Molony, "Existing-Home Sales
     Smash Record Again," July 25, 2005

18   American Dream Down payment Act of 2003, December 16,
     2003, www.consumer-
     guides.info/housing/Home_Owership/

19   Fred E. Foldvary, "Real Estate and Business Cycles: Henry
     George's Theory of the Trade Cycle"

20 Robert R Prechter Jr., Conquer the Crash, John Wiley and
    Sons, Ltd. 2002, Reproduced with permission

21 Bryan B Sterling and Frances N. Sterling, *Reflection and
    Observations, Crown*, 1982

22 Peter Slatin, "A Wicked Credit Crunch," www.forbes.com

23 Alan Greenspan, before the Senate Banking Committee,
    April 20, 2004

24 Alan Greenspan, before the Joint Economic Committee, May
    21, 2003

Chapter 4

1   Maury Klein, *Rainbow's End: The Crash of 1929*, Oxford
    University Press, 2001, p 142

2   Herbert Hoover, speech accepting the Republican
    nomination, Palo Alto, California.
    http://historymatters.gmu.edu/d/5063.html

3   Maury Klein, *Rainbow's End: The Crash of 1929*, Oxford
    University Press, 2001, p 158

4   H. B. Watkins, *The Hungry Years*, Henry Holt and Company,
    LLC,
    1999, p 10

5   Maury Klein, *Rainbow's End: The Crash of 1929*, Oxford
    University Press, 2001, p 12

6   Robert S. Mcelvanine, *The Great Depression*, Three Rivers
    Press, 1993, p 17

7   Karen Blumenthal, *Six Days In October: The Stock Market Crash of 1929*, Atheneum, 2002, p 13

8   ibid, p 19

9   ibid, pp 61, 62

10   Barbara Silberdick Feinberg, *Black Tuesday: The Stock Market Crash of 1929*, Millbrook Press, 1995, pp 7, 8

11   President Hoover, March 1930

12   H. B. Watkins, *The Hungry Years*, Henry Holt and Company, LLC,
     1999, p 55

13   Charles A. Jellison, *Tomatoes Were Cheaper: Tales from the Thirties*, Syracuse University Press, Syracuse, NY. 1977

14   H. B. Watkins, *The Hungry Years*, Henry Holt and Company, LLC,
     1999, p 61

15   Frederick Lewis Allen, *Since Yesterday*, Perennial-Harpercollins,
     July 1986

16   Welling@Weeden.com, Al Freidberg, March 23, 2001

17   Gotfried Von Haberier, *Prosperity and Depression*, University Press of the Pacific, 2001

18   Alvin H. Hansen, *Business Cycles and National Income*, W.W. Norton & Company, New York, 1964

"The reasonable man
adapts himself to the world.
The unreasonable man persists
in trying to adapt the world to himself.
Therefore, all progress depends on the
unreasonable man."

George Bernard Shaw
1935 Nobel prize winner
1856-1950

2092854

Made in the USA